Summertime Blues

Summertime Blues

Dublin's Epic Journey to a Historic All-Ireland

Roland Tormey

MAINSTREAM PUBLISHING

EDINBURGH AND LONDON

First published in Great Britain in 2007 by
MAINSTREAM PUBLISHING COMPANY
(EDINBURGH) LTD
7 Albany Street
Edinburgh EH1 3UG

ISBN 9781845963064

This book is a work of non-fiction based on the life, experiences
and recollections of the author. The author has stated to the
publishers that the contents of this book are true

All picture section photographs courtesy of Sportsfile
unless otherwise stated

A catalogue record for this book is available
from the British Library

Typeset in Bembo and Stone Informal

Printed in Great Britain by
William Clowes Ltd, Beccles, Suffolk

For Christine, Charlotte, Olivia and Kitty

Contents

Foreword
by Dessie Farrell 9

Prelude
Blue, Blue Day 11

One
Barstool Blues 17

Two
Worried Man Blues 37

Three
Blue Spanish Sky 69

Four
Me and the Devil Blues 91

Five
My Blue Heaven 107

Six
Red-Eyed and Blue 135

Seven
North Country Blues 163

Eight
Western Bound Blues 203

Acknowledgements 215

Notes 217

Sources Used 221

Foreword by Dessie Farrell

IT'S HARD TO BELIEVE that Dublin senior footballers have only won a single All-Ireland title in 24 years. Reared on a diet of success as a child of the 1970s, I first entered a Dublin dressing-room that, I believed, was merely biding its time. All-Irelands would follow.

However, what transpired was an almost traumatic journey to the ultimate goal in 1995. The most incredible series of near-misses ended for us that year in a blue wave of emotion – and the release, ironically, probably cost Dublin an All-Ireland the following year.

Whether it was just reward for the most consistent team of the early 1990s, other people can decide. I believed it was still only the start to a new period of All-Ireland glory for Dublin. What I was to learn subsequently is that sport can be a cruel mistress and that an All-Ireland medal is the most precious commodity of all.

Yet, now that I can take a step back, I realise that, besides the success, it was the most incredible period of our lives. We were privileged to have played with such a great squad, and the ability of men like Keith Barr, Paddy Moran, Mick Galvin, Charlie Redmond, Paul Curran and Jim Gavin to pick themselves up after the cruellest of defeats and go at it again was simply remarkable.

There were also the players who missed out when we did eventually cross the line – players like Jack Sheedy, Mick Kennedy and Eamon Heery – and their contribution to this story is as important as that of any who played in 1995.

Summertime Blues is a frighteningly accurate title for this wonderfully evocative story of the Dublin team in the 1990s. While it pains me to relive some of those too numerous memories of defeat, I am thankful that I was part of it all.

As time passes, the contribution of this Dublin team grows in stature, so long dwarfed by the triumphs of the 1970s. *Summertime Blues* is an account of one of the finest Dublin teams of the modern era, the last flag-bearers in a city starved of All-Ireland success.

Prelude – Blue, Blue Day

MEMORY PLAYS TRICKS ON you. Although I was there at the time, and saw it as it happened, my memory of the last-gasp penalty in the 1994 championship final is based on the television replays that I have seen over and over again, not on what I saw with my own eyes. My memory of the kick itself, that is. I can remember all of the wild tumult that was going on around me at the time, but my memory of what was happening on the pitch has been overwritten by often-viewed television pictures of those moments.

And yet, the seconds in which it all took place seemed to last an eternity, and I swear that at the time I thought they would be forever engrained on my memory. Tens of thousands of raw throats shouted in unison, 'Penalty! Jesus Fucking Christ Ref! Fucking Penalty!' The referee ran to the edge of the penalty square just in front of me and made that familiar cruciform gesture that signals a penalty in Gaelic games. I was directly behind the goal, crushed among the most hardcore of Dublin Gaelic football fans, and all around me the crowd erupted with ecstatic delight. I felt myself get picked up off my feet and dragged forward and then backward, buffeted about by the frenzied roaring of the sky-blue-and-navy sea of bodies as I scrambled frantically to get my feet back on solid concrete. For a second I was terrified – I could be crushed – but ecstatic too, and I grabbed hold of a stranger and shook him, and screamed a roar of anger and release. He slapped me hard, three or four times on the shoulder, in a gesture of violent solidarity, and then he was swept away on the ever-churning sea of bodies. With only minutes to go on the clock, Dublin were a goal down and had a penalty to draw level. Our opponents, Down, hadn't looked like scoring for the previous 20 minutes and if this penalty was scored there was only one team that would win. This penalty would give Dublin their first All-Ireland championship title in 11 years.

The crowd began to shush and settle and it was these quiet moments that seemed to last forever. The joyous release of the penalty award vanished with the shushing of the crowd, and the gnawing, knotted feeling in the pit of my gut returned. All the summer came down to this moment. Dublin had been playing championship matches since June and had played teams both mediocre and great to reach the promised land that was Croke Park on the third Sunday in September. On the morning of each of those matches – irrespective of the opposition – I had awoken with the same tight knot in my gut, my body telling me that it was a match day even before my brain knew I was awake. The award of the penalty had granted a momentary release, but now the anxiety returned with a vengeance. Whereas in soccer a penalty is more often than not a certain goal, in Gaelic football things are not so clear-cut. The penalty mark is further back than in soccer and the goal is slightly smaller. Missed penalties had contributed to Dublin's championship exits in 1988 and 1991 and had played a role in their losing of the 1992 championship final.

Significantly, Dublin's star dead-ball specialist, Charlie Redmond, had been responsible for his share of those missed penalties. So along with the hush that ran around the ground was the whispered question as to who would take the penalty. 'Not Charlie,' we said to ourselves and to whoever was listening, nearby or, indeed, above: 'Jesus, please. Not Charlie.' Charlie was, more than anyone else, responsible for Dublin being in the final. He had single-handedly dragged Dublin into a replay with a well-taken point deep in stoppage time when they seemed set to lose their first match of the season, and he had been one of the country's outstanding forwards all year. More than that, he had been a long-standing servant of Dublin football. Now playing in what many suspected might be his last match, he was one of only two players that formed a link back to the last Dublin side to win the championship, in 1983. He was also the archetypal Dub: a big, loud, sassy, street-smart, wise-cracking bastard, just the sort of fella we all admired. It wasn't just that we feared Charlie would miss – we did, but at the same time we remembered that he had also scored a penalty earlier in the season – it was that we feared for him too. We feared his vulnerability under pressure in front of goal, and we feared that the man who had brought us to this moment might be the one who would fuck it all up in these last few moments. 'Not Charlie,' we repeated. 'Jesus, please. Not Charlie.'

It was Charlie.

The greasy, wet ball was placed on the spot, and Charlie stood up to take the penalty in front of the blue sea of bodies on Hill 16 and in front of all of Croke Park, packed to the rafters with almost 59,000 people. From the substitutes' bench, Ciaran Walsh looked on in trepidation. Walsh had been a key part of Dublin's last line of defence throughout the previous few years and should have played a central role in marshalling one of the most feared attacks in the country. Unfortunately, however, a hip injury had cruelly ruled him out of contention for the final. Instead, Dublin had been forced to improvise and play a non-specialist in Walsh's position. The experiment had been a disaster and Down had prospered early on, running into a substantial lead before Dublin began to haul them back in. As the game unfolded in front of him, Walsh's mind swam with one desperate phrase, repeated over and over again: 'I should be out there, I should be out there.' Had he been fit and able to play it was unlikely that Dublin would have been in the position of needing a penalty to level the game with eight minutes to go. They were, however. Now it was up to Charlie.

His shot was low and to the right of the goalkeeper, but never good enough. The keeper got down well and the ball rebounded into the square. Charlie later recalled, 'As the ball came back out I still thought I could get to it. I was trying to work out should I just tap it in or should I catch it first and then tap it in. I decided to catch it, but a couple of players – I think it was D.J. Kane and Johnny Barr – arrived, and the ball was knocked out and that was it.'

It shouldn't have all been over, but it was. Dublin still had eight minutes to get the three points they needed to draw the game level, but as that ball trickled wide the confidence that had been growing in them left with an almost audible whoosh. In the frantic minutes between the penalty and the final whistle, Dublin laid siege to the Down goal, but none of the forwards seemed able to connect with each other. Dublin shot wide time after time, and their reward for all the frantic pressure was a single point. The final whistle sounded: Down had won by two points.

We stood on Hill 16, bewildered and hurting. Some shouted their disapproval at the referee or at the tactics of the Down team; others hurled abuse at their own team; and yet more stormed off the terrace as quickly as they could. Most simply stood, unable to make sense of what had just happened but ready to clap both the Dubs and the winning team. Most of the Down players came to exchange respectful salutes with the Dublin fans, but one pulled his jersey across his face and skipped along the front of the terrace making fuck-you two-fingered gestures at the Dublin fans. We half-heartedly shouted our disapproval. Why would someone do that? Was winning not enough? Did you have to see the opponents suffer, too? And then we stood and waited and clapped weakly as Down collected the Sam Maguire trophy for the second time in three years.

As we walked back into town from Croke Park, we shook our heads, said little and worked to fight the feelings of weary despair that kept welling up inside. We had played every second of the game with the lads on the pitch, and we were exhausted. We had been so close.

'Charlie won't be back after that. He'll definitely retire,' said someone. We just shook our heads, half in disagreement, half in resignation.

Someone else, trying to lift the mood said, 'Next year . . .' but instead of cheering us up, that just pissed us off. Dublin had been so close for so long. We had lost the championship final in 1992, lost the semi-final to the eventual champions by a single point in 1993 and now lost the 1994 final by two points. The chance to win an All-Ireland title was not easy to come by, and winning was not a birthright. You can't fail to take three chances and expect to get a fourth. Suddenly it hit me.

'Jesus!' I said, 'I will never see Dublin win an All-Ireland.' And at that moment, I believed that it was true.

One

Barstool Blues

THREE YEARS PREVIOUSLY, IN the late summer of 1991, Dublin footballers were regretting another penalty miss that had put them out of the championship, and I was sitting at the bar of the Irish Times pub in Washington DC. Sitting beside me, also on his own, was an elderly American man nursing a beer. I was keeping to myself, reading a book while I waited for my friends to arrive, but the elderly gent beside me had other ideas. 'Lost all the games in the pre-season,' he barked at me, in a thick, almost impenetrable, accent.

'Huh?' I grunted at him.

'Redskins!' he exclaimed with force, his eyebrows rising like Yosemite Sam's eyebrows in a Donald Duck cartoon. 'Lost all the games in the pre-season.'

'Not looking good, huh?' I ventured.

'Ha! Last time that happened, Vince Lombardi came to town!' The way in which he nodded and smiled at this last statement led me to believe that he felt (a) that this was an utterance of sage-like significance, and (b) that only an idiot would not understand its significance. Unfortunately for me, I was that idiot.

On the one hand, I knew enough to know that the Redskins were the Washington Redskins, the local 'gridiron' (American football) team. On the other hand, I had not followed their progress in the pre-season. Nor did I know who Vince Lombardi was or the significance of his visiting a locality. Logically, since playing poorly had previously given rise to a visit from Mr Lombardi, this could mean that he was the guy who awarded the booby prize to the team that finished last. Common sense therefore dictated that my next comment should be about how, with luck and a long season, they might turn things around. At the same time, I knew enough to know that it was dangerous to apply logic to sporting conversations since often the purpose of such conversations is to show to other people that your knowledge of the arcane vagaries of sporting lore is such that you can predict when sport defies all logic. If this was one of those conversations, the use of logic could mark me out as a moron. Confessing my ignorance was not an option since his countenance made clear that this too would mark me down as an idiot. Having quickly weighed my options, I did the only thing I could do: I said, 'Ah!' and nodded and smiled in what I hoped was a knowledgeable and enigmatic manner.

The ruse worked. The old guy nodded along and grinned a broad, toothless grin. He began to gush forth with the stories and rumours of the forthcoming season, and, like a skilled fortune-teller swirling tea leaves in the bottom of a china cup, he picked over the bones of each story and pronounced on their significance. All it needed was an occasional nod or a grunt from me to keep him going. It turned out that I had done well not to trust logic. The Vince Lombardi in question was the Vince Lombardi Trophy, the NFL Championship trophy – the US equivalent of Gaelic football's Sam Maguire trophy or soccer's Jules Rimet trophy. He had been telling me that the last time the Redskins had lost all the matches of the pre-season they went on to win the championship. Although logic would see this as a weak basis on which to be basing confident predictions for the forthcoming season, my elderly and toothless friend was adamant – this would be the Redskins' year. (It later turned out that, whatever its dubious basis, his prediction was right: the Redskins did indeed beat the Buffalo Bills in the Super Bowl the following winter.)

His monologue on sports was wide ranging and he exhibited a prodigious knowledge of American sports, but his passion on that day was gridiron football because it was that time of year. To him, sports were like the calendar: they were the basis on which his own body clock ticked. While other people woke up in the morning knowing it was July, he woke up knowing it was the baseball season and that the Orioles were at home for a double-header. When other people were putting up new calendars and singing 'Auld Lang Syne', he was arguing the outcome of the upcoming Super Bowl.

People like that guy can be found all around the world, people for whom sport is the basis on which they connect with other people and the way in which they measure the passing of days. In Ireland, such people often use Gaelic games as the clock against which the summer is measured. Starting in February, in schools, workplaces, bars and homes throughout the country, stories, myths and rumours begin to circulate about the form of different players and teams in the run-up to the championship season. Someone is flying in training. Someone else is carrying a knee injury. The new young lad coming through played well in a closed-doors challenge match against one of the top teams. One of the senior members of the squad has had a falling out with the manager over the training routines. All the stories are dissected, analysed, weighed and digested, and each rumour passes like the grains in a sand clock, measuring the growing tension and anticipation and counting down the time until late May or early June arrives, your team plays their first-round game and the summer begins.

Many of these springtime predictions are based on the performance of each team in the National League which, in the mid-1990s, took place over the winter and spring of each year. The National League competition was then, as now, regarded as being of secondary importance to the championship, but it provided a good opportunity for teams to test themselves against other teams while they were training for the beginning of the championship season. At the time, doing well in the league was regarded as a mixed blessing, because the later stages of the league took place around the beginning of the championship season, and a successful run to the league final could leave a team tired at the time of year they needed to be approaching their peak. Sometimes winning the league could give a team a confidence boost, but, more often than not, a place in the league final was regarded as a poisoned chalice. Generally, most of the big teams wanted to avoid relegation to a lower division and, if possible, make it to the knockout stages of the competition, but as a rule they then seemed happy enough to be knocked out so they could concentrate on the summer.

Based on Dublin's 1994–95 league form, the forthcoming championship was unlikely to give rise to a vintage year for the Dubs. After their narrow defeat in the previous year's All-Ireland final, the Dublin team had, it seemed, gone to pieces. Their early league form had been poor, losing most of their games, and they had reached the last two games with relegation from the top division more a likelihood than a possibility. Although they put up a better showing in those final two games, a win against Down and a draw against Derry were not enough to avoid the drop: Dublin would be playing football in the lower divisions the following year. Many people suggested that the team had been around the top too long and now lacked the hunger to keep winning.

By the mid-1990s the core of the team had been around the block together for half a decade, and this gave them a sense of togetherness that was not always evident in other teams. While there were, of course, the same personality clashes and cliques that one might find in other teams, there was also a strong sense of camaraderie. As Keith Barr later recalled, 'We had a funny relationship with one another in that team. We all loved one another, and we cared for one another, but at the same time we wouldn't think twice about fucking one another out of it. Or we wouldn't think twice about hitting one another a slap in training. The respect we had for one another was of the utmost, but if anybody stepped out of line, they were fairly quickly put back into it and that wasn't done by talking or chatting. It would be done on the training field with a slap or a dirty tackle. So that's the type of body language we used towards one another.'

In a way, this closeness probably made it difficult for new players to break into the side. In the dressing-room, many players had their own spot, with the more established lads sitting furthest from the management and those less established being left to the seats nearest the management or, on occasion, being left standing. New players were also often viewed with a sense of caution, as the older hands watched them to see if they would make the grade and become accepted, or if instead they would slip away and become one of the many who passed through but didn't quite have what it took. If they did stick around, however, they became part of the group, and they, like the rest, would find themselves looking forward to training not just because they were getting fitter and better but also because they were among friends. Central to this group were a bunch of characters who brought a swaggering attitude to Gaelic football. From John O'Leary, the ever-solid and outspoken captain and goalkeeper at the back, through the totally committed and often unpredictable Keith Barr in defence, to the big, cocky, brash and vulnerable Charlie Redmond in attack, the Dublin team had more than a few players who were larger than life.

Central to the squad was the captain, John O'Leary. O'Leary was the one Dublin player remaining who knew what it was like to win an All-Ireland medal on the pitch (Charlie Redmond had been a substitute in 1983). A building society manager by day, on championship Sundays he became the lean figure who dominated his goal and the space in front of it, who had won almost every honour in Gaelic football and who had been chosen as the All-Star goalkeeper for the previous two seasons. Unafraid of the physical aspects of the game and displaying the kind of hardiness that makes Gaelic football fans scoff at the sight of soccer players rolling around the pitch after the slightest nudge, he had repeatedly lined out for Dublin while carrying injuries and, by 1995, had represented Dublin consistently for 15 years without missing a single championship game. In 1994, he had dislocated a finger in training the day before the provincial final. Looking at the mess that was his hand, for a moment he worried that the injury might keep him out of the game. But, with the help of the team's manager, he snapped the damaged finger back into place and the following day lined out once more.

O'Leary was one-quarter of the last line of defence made up of himself and the three men in the full-back line in front of him. Together they operated a defensive system that was one of the meanest in the country. O'Leary was constantly talking, calling warnings to the men in front of him and ensuring that they were well organised. The four had built up an instinctive understanding of each other that allowed them to mesh seamlessly. Fans often get excited by spectacular blocks or saves, but the Dublin defensive system was not spectacular insofar as it was based on doing the simple things well. It was, nonetheless, hugely effective. Because it was not spectacular, the other three – Paddy Moran, Dermot Deasy and Ciaran Walsh – often did not receive the same plaudits as did O'Leary, but nonetheless the four worked as a close unit covering each other, plugging gaps and breaking down attacks before they threatened to turn into goals. They were a close unit that socialised together as well as played together and helped to give O'Leary the platform to put in All-Star performances as goalkeeper year after year.

O'Leary took his role as captain very seriously. He sought to play a strong part in motivating the team and individual players. He was one of those that always worked to ensure that new young players did not become overawed at the thought of breaking into the senior championship squad. At the same time, he was never shy about telling the manager if he felt that a particular player did not have what it took to make it. In public, O'Leary carried a quiet authority. His words always seemed well chosen, his judgements insightful, and he was thought of by many as a future manager of the Dubs. In the private world of the squad, however, he was one of the court jesters, one of those who enlivened the team and made it a place fellas wanted to belong to and wanted to stay. He was a master at winding people up and there seemed to be no limits to what he would do in order to effect a gag. If someone arrived back in the car park after a hard training session to find that the wheels of his car had been stolen, chances were that O'Leary was behind the stunt. The targeted player would get more and more frantic while the others feigned surprise and concern until eventually the squad would dissolve into a fit of laughter and the wheels would reappear.

By 1995, however, O'Leary had been Dublin's only choice as championship goalkeeper for a decade and a half and some wondered if, after the wear and tear of all those years, he could summon his energy for one more tilt at the title. Dublin had been using a sports psychologist for the previous few years – something that seemed to many people out of place in the macho world of Gaelic football – and the psychological fallout of coming so close so often and yet failing to reach the summit was a concern for the fans. While Johno was thought to be amongst the more tough-minded of the team, we wondered if the hunger and the drive would still be there.

At the far end of the pitch from John O'Leary (geographically and, it seemed, psychologically) was Charlie Redmond. Like Johno, Charlie seemed to have been part of the Dublin set-up forever. He had played a few games in the 1983 All-Ireland winning season, coming on as a substitute on two occasions that year before finally establishing himself as a match-starting player in 1985. While John O'Leary's day job was in the sedate middle-class world of financial management, Charlie worked in the rather more physical and macho world of firefighting. Firefighters live in a world where they have to be willing to go out the door when the bell rings without knowing if they are going to face a cat in a tree or the Towering Inferno. In order to cope, they often develop a sort of testosterone-fuelled, devil-may-care attitude that says to the world, 'Bring it on!' The attitude seemed to fit Charlie perfectly. He walked with a swagger that most young men would love to have emulated, and, in public, he carried a sharp Dublin wit which meant that a wise-cracking quip was never far away.

By the mid-1990s Charlie was Dublin's dead-ball specialist, a point-kicking metronome who seemed able to swing the ball over the bar from almost any point on the pitch within 50 metres of the posts. Charlie had been influenced in his peculiar ritual for free-taking by the New Zealand rugby player Grant Fox, and whether Dublin were a point down or ten points in front, the ritual never changed. He placed the ball on the ground, took seven steps backward, three to the side and then stood for a moment, gazing at the distant posts. He then licked the fingers of his hand and slowly wiped them across his chest, once, twice, then a third time, before shuffling sideways towards the ball, picking up speed and finally launching the ball in an arc that always seemed heading wide of the posts, before, inevitably, curling in to register a point. The significance of the hand licking was never clear to anyone else, and many questioned how sanitary his ritual was, but, whatever its health implications, it was effective: Charlie rarely missed frees, irrespective of the pressure on the kick.

Of course, as we had seen to our cost, the same could not be said of penalty-kicks, and this was part of the curious conundrum of the man. While Charlie walked with a brash and wonderfully arrogant swagger, he also appeared vulnerable to dark moments of self-doubt at crucial times. All of which meant that in the spring of 1995 questions were being asked about the future of Charlie Redmond. It was not the first time that questions had been asked about him. When Dublin got to the league final in early 1993, Charlie seemed to be sluggish and overweight, and compounded a poor performance by getting himself sent off for a couple of tired-looking tackles. Added to his penalty miss in the previous year's championship final, the consensus among the fans leaving Croke Park that league final day was that we had seen the last of Charlie Redmond in a Dublin jersey. Yet, Charlie had fought his way back and, although the 1993 championship season had started without him, he was back in the team by June and was back in the starting line-up by July. The question we were asking was whether he had the mental toughness and the will to come back again, after all the roller-coaster years and after the sickening finale to the previous year's All-Ireland final.

Charlie had thought about retiring from Dublin football after the 1994 final. He had planned that, if Dublin won, he would go out on a high. Reality took a different path, however, and he ended up fleeing from Croke Park after the final whistle, rushing out of the dressing-room without even taking a shower, tears streaming down his face. As he sat in the traffic outside the stadium, trying to get away, bunches of fans streamed past his car, oblivious to his presence.

'Poor Charlie,' said one.

'Poor Charlie?' queried another. 'Fuck Charlie!'

The two walked on, not knowing that they had brought a smile to the face of the subject of their discussion. The smile didn't mean that the tough times were over, though. Throughout the shortening days of autumn and into the dank, dark, never-ending nights of winter, Charlie had been tortured with the memory of the failed penalty that he felt had cost Dublin the championship. He would later reflect that 'unless you lose an All-

Ireland as a player, no one can ever prepare you for how bad you feel and no one understands how bad you feel'. Charlie blamed himself for the loss of the final (although there was no doubt that many other decisions on and off the pitch had contributed to the loss). He later recalled, 'I went through a lot of personal turmoil because I had missed penalties in All-Ireland finals two years out of three: 1992 was bad but we had all played bad that day; 1994 was different because we had played well, and it was the penalty miss that had lost the game, and I was going to have to live with that. It was quite a burden to live with it.' That he had the sympathy of the nation was no help; indeed, it was unbearable to have absolute strangers walk up to him on the street to wish him luck, that gesture of kindness tearing at the raw and open wound that he still carried.

Although he had thought of retirement after the 1994 final, in the aftermath of the penalty save, as he had stood in the square in front of Hill 16 with the world coming apart all around him and with a torrent of emotions coursing through him, one thought came clearly to mind: 'It can't end this way. Not after all this time.' And so, when the team reassembled for training that winter, Charlie had returned, driven by the need for one more season to bring redemption.

If Charlie was driven that year by the need to exorcise the demons of the previous September, Keith Barr was, it seemed, simply driven. Barr had broken into the Dublin team in 1989 and had quickly established himself as an ever-present fixture in the Dublin half-back line. He was a stocky, physically strong and aggressive player, and Dublin had struggled for a while to find the best place to deploy his talents. He had been tried in the half-forward line for a while before being shifted back to half-back, where he could anchor the play, cut off opposition attacks as they were building, and drive forward to join the Dublin attack when necessary. By 1994 the Dublin trio of Paul Curran, Mick Deegan and Keith Barr were regarded as the best half-back line in the country, as much for their contributions in attack as for their rock-steady defence. Their tendency to tear up field and abandon their defensive posts had, however, cost Dublin on occasion and, by 1995, they were working on a more measured approach to balancing attack and defence. Curran and Deegan could still burst forward carrying the ball up the wings to join the attack, but Barr would restrain himself and use his vision and his passing ability to distribute the ball and make plays in much the same way as an American football quarterback.

If John O'Leary appeared thoughtful and analytical, and Charlie appeared brilliant and troubled, Keith appeared to be all heart and guts. While there was no doubt that he was a skilful and intelligent footballer, his key attribute was the 'Death or Glory' attitude he seemed to bring to all big encounters. Yet the aggression that was so central to Barr's game was not always channelled to productive uses. In the 1989 championship semi-final he had reacted badly to a Cork player's goading and his sending-off that day contributed to losing the match for Dublin. In the 1993 league final he had launched a bizarre and spectacular gazelle leap into a scrum of players and could easily have hurt a member of either team or, indeed, himself. (Needless to say, like Charlie Redmond, he was also sent off that day.) While other Dublin players were often respected as ball players, Keith was not well loved by opposing fans, many of whom thought of him as nothing more than a brutish thug. Not that we cared what they thought. Keith was one of us – he connected with the Dublin fans in a visceral way and his whole manner seemed to say that he would die for, or – preferably – kill for, the Dublin jersey.

Like O'Leary, Keith was one of the characters of the squad, one of those who brought a sense of mischief to the set-up. If fellow teammates found the arse had been cut out of their shorts, or the toes from their stockings, Keith would be one of those suspected. Someone might open their kit bag to find that a pair of women's knickers had been deposited on top of their gear and, in the slagging that followed, Keith would be centrally involved.

While Keith had not played at the top level for as long as John O'Leary or Charlie Redmond, questions remained. The previous few years had been a roller-coaster ride of heart-stopping highs and gut-wrenching lows, marked by a continued failure to close out a game while in a winning position. No one doubted the ability of the team, though more than a few doubted whether they had the mental toughness and discipline to be winners. When we looked back at the preceding few years we wondered whether they had been moving ever closer to the ultimate goal, or whether, like a tide that has already turned, they had passed their high-water mark and were now, slowly and imperceptibly, but inexorably, in decline.

But, while there were a lot of questions hanging over the team in the spring of 1995, there were also a few hopeful signs. The Dubs had performed well in the last few games of the league campaign and this could be seen as an indication that they had shaken off their lethargy. Much discussion also centred on the hope that some of the off-season's new arrivals had strengthened the team. Throughout the 1994 season we had filed into Croke Park early in order to catch some part of the underage championship match that was played before the senior teams took to the field. Dublin had been without significant underage success for some time but the 1994 team gave us hope for the future. They played with panache and drive, and it seemed that any number of players from that team might one day make the senior panel. The most exciting of all was Jason Sherlock. Sherlock had announced himself to us on the day of the 1994 Leinster final by scorching across Croke Park's green turf like a comet midway through the second half and crashing the ball into the back of the net for the decisive score. In a couple of years, we thought, when he has put on enough muscle to take the big hits of the senior game and, if the extra weight hasn't slowed him down too much, that young lad could do well for the Dubs. But Jason didn't have a few years to wait. That winter he had been called up for the senior team, and, although the team as a whole had not given us much cause for confidence, some who had seen him play during the league suggested that the previous summer's exploits were not those of a one-hit wonder.

By the time he made the breakthrough into the Dublin football team, Jason was an accomplished soccer player and hurler, and had represented Ireland at underage basketball. Although most people's stereotype of a basketball player is someone who looks like they have been reared putting Human Growth Hormone on their cornflakes instead of milk, the diminutive Jason had dribbled and passed his way through his lanky fellow players and had finished top scorer the year he played in the All-Ireland schools' basketball final. It was his exploits playing professional soccer in the League of Ireland, however, that suggested this short and slight kid could indeed hold his own against heavily built men twice his age and laden with violent intent.

Jason's skin marked him out as well as his skill. Although Ireland had had people of colour grab the public imagination before, Jason was not Phil Lynott or Paul McGrath, because the young kid with Asian features was playing Gaelic football not playing bass guitar in a rock band or playing soccer. Racism had played its part in developing his character, both on the streets of Finglas and on the fields of play in north Cork. Some suspected that race had even played a role in the failure of Cork to grasp the talent that was in their midst before he was snatched up by his home county of Dublin. There had been a time when he reacted with aggression to the petty nastiness that was sometimes used to target him and to break his concentration, but he had learned to turn his anger inwards, to ignore the provocations and to answer them through his play.

Of course, Jason seemed too small and too young and we

feared what might happen to him in the heat of a championship summer. At 175 cm (5 ft 9 in.) tall and 67 kg (147 lb) in weight, he was not only the shortest player on the team but also over 10 kg (22 lb) lighter than any other player on the Dublin team. Irish soccer may well have had its share of bruising characters but it was routine in Gaelic football for a player to be 'welcomed' to the game with a punch or two early on and we had all seen occasions where a player was floored before the ball had even been thrown in. Jason's speed and exuberance would certainly add a welcome zest to the Dublin attack but we feared what sort of damage might be done to him – and to the team's prospects – in the white fury that was championship football by some meaty defender who would know from experience that it would be hard for the kid to score against you if he was lying on the turf holding his face in agony.

In the spring of 1995, therefore, neither we nor some of our team were confident. Although the fans looking on did not know it, a heavy veil of quiet desperation had descended around some of the Dublin team during the winter of 1994–95. The beginning of training each season is always psychologically hard, as the players find themselves on dark evenings running endlessly while the skin on their bare arms, legs and faces is whipped raw by stinging needles of pelting rain. And while some approached 1995 much like any other year, for others this season seemed harder than ever. They had become frustrated by their repeated stumbling so close to the winning line and, as they faced the new season, the horror of another potential failure hung heavily over them. In late January and early February, players who had been taking a break during the early stages of the league began to drift back to training. Some were well above their target weight and a number of the older players were still considering whether or not they would actually play in the 1995 season. Some of the good humour and vivacity that characterised and bonded the Dublin squad seemed to have been drained away.

They had been struggling through training for a few weeks, all the time with the fear that some of the senior players might drift away hanging over them, when someone suggested they go out together for a meal and a few drinks. It turned out to be a crucial decision. That night, the buzz started to come back. As their sense of camaraderie slowly returned so did their motivation. Players looked around and saw that the old guard was still standing, and they too decided to give it a go for another year. This year a different approach was taken to training, as there was a feeling that the league should not be allowed to interfere with the championship preparation. Dublin had, after all, done well in the league over the previous few years but this had always meant nothing when it came to the championship shake-up. Weight training became part of the regime for the first time, and the new approach to training helped to make it clear to the players that the focus was on being right for the championship season. The team's psychologist played a role in this renewed motivation too. They were 'the nearly men', they were told. Their exploits over the previous few years had changed the course of Gaelic games but, as things stood, they had no place in the record books. Without an All-Ireland title they would be remembered, if at all, as one of the great losing sides of all time. The words stuck in the team's imagination. They did not want to be the nearly men. They would give it one last shot.

* * *

The lack of confidence we and some of our team felt in the spring of 1995 was more than simply a discussion point, more than something to be mulled over with colleagues during the lunch break while waiting for the kettle to boil. It cut to the very essence of what it meant to be Dubs, because we Dubs did not simply want to win, we expected to. We were the city slickers, the metropolitans. When looking for kinship, we turned not to the drab and narrow streets of Waterville or Clonmel but to those who, like us, lived in a sprawling and important metropolis. Our kinship was with Mancunians, Liverpudlians,

New Yorkers, Londoners; sometimes, if the mood took us and the weather was good, maybe even Parisians. Navan may have only been up the road, but psychologically it was a different country and not one you would want to visit on holiday. Even other Irish places that made claims to be a part of the Universal Brotherhood of Cities did not fit into our reckoning. Cork, for all its size and people, had its claim to citydom fatally compromised by the fact that its association with such essentially backward and rural places as Skibbereen and Clonakilty dragged it back into the bog. Indeed, while Cork's claim to citydom was at least arguable, it seemed that every over-sized village in Ireland from Kilkenny to Limerick was claiming city status. The fact that all these places were smaller than a good-sized Dublin suburb was sufficient to ensure that, however long they claimed to have had their charter, we knew they weren't part of the great and sophisticated metropolitan 'us'.

So, like city people everywhere, we understood that we were the best. After all, if Dublin was not the best, why did all of the country folk spend their every waking moment working to get out of where they were and 'up' to Dublin? (Every now and again, someone would try to answer this question with reference to differential patterns of economic development, brought about by the policies of the Dublin-based government, but we ignored such pedantic responses: the question was rhetorical.) This self-confidence was essential to our self-understanding: Dubs walked with a swagger and were smart talking and quick quipping. We started each race as a winner.

This self-confidence had long been part of the Dublin football psyche. When the former Dublin star Paddy Cullen was appointed manager of the side in the early 1990s, he brought a 'We're Dubs, we need to take our guns from our holsters and blow these culchies away' style to the team. Having spent years with a Dublin team that was good enough to beat almost anybody without trying too hard, Paddy seemed not to worry too much about tactics but resorted instead to telling the team that it was their job to keep men with tractors in their place. Indeed, in the run-up to the 1992 championship final, Paddy appeared not to have over-concerned himself with preparation either, perhaps unable to countenance the idea that the Dubs might be beaten. The Dubs were beaten that day, but initially at least, that didn't affect our belief that every match was there for the winning. When the Dublin crowd on Hill 16 was in full voice it was as much in frustration that Dublin were even being required to play the opposition as it was in support of the team: 'Come on, Dubs, you're much better than this lot,' we would roar. 'What the fuck are you doing, Dubs! Jesus! Put this shower away and let's go home.' Our arrogance meant that when we turned on Dub-mode no one else liked us, but we didn't care. That was the way it had to be: after all, the provincial French hated the arrogant Parisians, who in turn pitied their backward rural brethren, while Texans and New Yorkers regarded each other as foreigners. Who were we to try to change the essential order of things? People from 'the country' would always hate the Dubs, but we weren't there to make friends. We were there to win, and, in doing so, confirm the everlasting superiority of our modern lives over the muck-scratching existence of those who didn't yet live in the city – not *a* city, but *the* city.

But the time for being comfortable in our arrogance and in the enmity of the rest of the country was past. On Hill 16, we had grown increasingly desperate as the Dubs had repeatedly come close but failed to close the deal. Our songs and chants had, in the past, always mirrored the self-assurance of our team: 'We are the Dubs – the D-U-B-S,' we sang, 'When the Dubs go up to collect the Sam Maguire, we'll be there, we'll be there.' For us it had not been a question of 'if' we collected the trophy, but of 'when'. By 1994, that optimism was draining away and the Dublin wits had already amended this chant to give it a darker reading: 'When the Dubs go up to collect the Sam Maguire, we'll be dead, we'll be dead,' they sang, meaning it as a joke but feeling it nonetheless. By the spring of 1995, people felt sorry for us. In newspapers, columnists from other counties wrote that Dublin now 'deserved' to win an All-Ireland championship. Dublin had been the pre-eminent team of the early 1990s, they said, and it would be cruel of fate to deny them their place in the record books. We agreed, and we latched on to every positive word as a talisman that might ward off the evil spirits that had blighted our path to victory on previous occasions, but we hated them for it too. We hated that when they wished us luck they patronised us and we feared that their condescension might well be justified.

While we picked apart the Dubs and searched cravenly for any positive sign, we also watched the opposition to see who it was that might stand in our way. Largely we ignored the west of the country where football seemed in terminal decline. We were confident that whoever came out of the west could be defeated. The south of the country was a different matter. While Kerry, the eternal greats of Gaelic football, seemed mired in a decade-long funk, they had in Maurice Fitzgerald one of the most gifted Gaelic footballers of any generation. A man who seemed withdrawn and ill at ease in interviews off the pitch was in his element in the space inside the white lines, and once set loose on the green field he moved with an easy grace. There were times it seemed there was nothing he couldn't do with a football. Maurice was regularly singled out for physical ill-treatment on the pitch by opposing players who sought to counter his natural talent by chopping him down, yet he seemed to possess an almost unnaturally serene disposition. Where any other player would have reacted to such violence with retribution, Maurice tended to pick himself up and walk away. But this trait, admirable in itself, caused a football public with an – at best – ambivalent attitude to discipline to ask questions about his temperament. While no one doubted his elegant grace on the pitch, Kerry people wondered whether he had the strength of character necessary to drag his team to victory.

Perhaps a more realistic challenger from the south that year was Cork. Blending youth and experience, Cork had big names throughout the pitch. From Niall Cahalane in defence, through the San-Francisco-born Danny Culloty, who had learned his football skills practising with his father in Golden Gate Park, to the subtle brilliance of Larry Tompkins up front, Cork had talent throughout their side. Like Dublin, however, Cork had been close to a championship title on previous occasions – they had been beaten semi-finalists the previous year and beaten finalists the year before that, and, like Dublin, some wondered if their best days were not behind them.

Closer to home in the east, Meath were Dublin's greatest worry. Although Dublin had beaten Meath in the championship the two previous years, each victory had been carved out by a single point. In fact, if one totalled the aggregate scores over the previous six championship meetings between Dublin and Meath, the Dubs were in front by a single point (there had been three drawn games, Meath had won in 1991 by a single point and Dublin had won the matches in 1993 and 1994, each time by a single point). Like all matches between near neighbours, Dublin–Meath games had a special quality, a ferocious intensity where familiarity bred contempt and each team was happy to display that contempt on the field of play. If Dublin got through to the Leinster final, it was, in all likelihood, Meath that they would face.

Then there was Ulster. While Munster in the south and Leinster in the east might both put forward a reasonably strong candidate for championship honours, everyone knew that the teams from the province of Ulster had taken the championship in a stranglehold in the early 1990s and that they did not seem ready to relinquish their grip. Ulster football was often not pretty but it was effective. Eschewing the traditional game of catching and kicking, Ulster teams did not so much play matches as plunge themselves into a cauldron of rage from which only one team would emerge. It was often joked that it was so tough to win in Ulster that one year no team would win. But the intensity of Ulster football had, in recent years, become like the fire of a blacksmith's forge, and the team that emerged intact from that flame was stronger for having survived. For that reason, whoever survived Ulster's fratricidal contest would assume the mantle of favourites for the championship.

Derry had won the championship in 1993, and were a good side that played cleverly and to their strengths and could not be discounted. Tyrone, like Kerry, were graced by a footballing genius. Peter Canavan was an all-round footballer with pace, agility and the ability to kick well with either his right or left foot. Canavan was tough and brave too and although he was small (about the same height as Jason Sherlock) and was often targeted for aggressive treatment by players who lacked his ability, he seemed to take it in his stride.

But if Derry had structure and Tyrone had genius, the side that seemed to have it all was Down. Having won the All-Ireland title in 1991 and 1994, no one would sensibly bet against Down taking a third title in 1995. They were a well-balanced team with steel in defence and midfield and, in Mickey Linden and James McCartan, they had gifted players who were lethal if given half an opportunity in front of the posts. Down had experienced similar league form to Dublin, and this had led some to suggest that they had spent too long celebrating and not long enough preparing for the defence of their title. But it was also arguable that the league had enabled them to get the championship hangover out of their system and that they would be back stronger and ready.

And so, in May 1995, as the days lengthened and we looked to the summer with hope and growing expectation, many people began to install Down as favourites to lift the All-Ireland championship title in September of that year. But on Sunday, 21 May, the opening day of the championship, Down were knocked out, and the championship was blown wide open.

Two

Worried Man Blues

THE WEDNESDAY FOLLOWING DOWN'S early exit from the championship I suffered what could loosely be termed a sporting injury: I slipped a disc while watching a soccer match, the European Champions League final between Ajax Amsterdam and AC Milan. The game itself had been a dull affair, notable only for the fact that it was the last match in Frank Rijkaard's glittering playing career and for the introduction on the European stage of the teenage substitute Patrick Kluivert, who won the game with a toe-poked goal five minutes from time. Midway through the second half, while slouched on the sofa, I sneezed, and in that second I felt something go in my back. My whole body seized up immediately and I felt as if a burning needle had been jabbed into the base of my spine.

Unwilling to drag myself away from even such a dull game, and stupidly convinced that nothing as innocuous as a sneeze could have done any major damage, I lay on the sofa, grinding my teeth and twitching in agony until the game was over. Slowly, I made my way to bed, imagining that I would feel better in the morning. It was only when I woke the following morning that I knew I was in serious trouble. Every movement in any part of my body brought with it a juddering, grating pain in my lower back. I had slipped a disc twice before, and each time it had hurt, but it was always discomfort that I could live with. This was something else entirely. No pain I had ever felt compared to this.

I knew I needed help, but this posed a problem. I had recently got my first real job, and, as a result, had managed to move out of home. I had been sharing a house with two guys, but, only the previous week, a woman had moved in. Despite the pain, I did not quite feel that one of our first meetings should consist of her finding me in my boxer shorts on the upstairs landing, writhing in agony. It was true this was not your normal first-week-in-a-house situation, but I still felt something less exposed might be more appropriate as a get-to-know-you ice-breaker. It took me almost 15 minutes to get out of bed and put on a pair of jeans. By that stage, I was damp with sweat. I made it out of the bedroom and onto the upstairs landing. I called to see if anyone was in the house and was met with silence. I was, it seemed, on my own. It took me another ten minutes to get down the stairs. As I dragged myself grunting and panting down the stairs, I had time to think through my options. I lived only ten minutes' walk from a hospital, but there wasn't a chance in hell that I would ever make it there on foot. Needless to say, my motorbike was also out of the question. I should, of course, have called an ambulance, but for some reason I didn't even consider it. With my brain barely functioning, I called a taxi and went outside to wait. There I stood hunched over in the driveway, in the lightly falling drizzle, unable to stand up or to sit down while I waited for the cab to arrive.

The hospital was a blur. I was ushered quickly through the waiting masses in the Accident and Emergency department, and for the first time I began to realise that this was something to be taken seriously. I remember thinking how kind everyone was with me while I twitched and writhed. They prodded and poked for a while, then gave me a painkilling shot before sending me for an X-ray. An adult wheelchair could not be found, so I was loaded into a child's wheelchair, and, with my feet dragging along the ground under the chair, a porter pushed me to the lift. By the time I came out of the X-ray they had found a trolley for me, and, feeling a bit embarrassed about the drama of it all, I watched the ceiling tiles and overhead lights flash past as they wheeled me back to the A & E. Once there, I was loaded up with a sheaf of prescriptions and an instruction to take three weeks off work. I was then dispatched to a different part of the hospital to make an appointment to see a back specialist. Since I was a public patient with no medical insurance, the appointment was fixed for six months later, by which time we both knew I would either be permanently crippled or already cured. Afterwards, I stood in the doorway of the Accident and Emergency department, looking out at the gently falling rain and trying to figure out what to do. I realised quickly that there was only one course of action open to a red-blooded Irish male in such circumstances: I called my mammy and asked her could I come home to stay for a few weeks.

By the time that Louth and Kildare took to the field the following Sunday, I was back in my mother's house, stoned on Valium, laid out on the flat of my back and twitching in occasional spasms of agony. But, insofar as it was possible to get excited about anything in my drugged-up state, I was excited about Kildare's game with Louth. Results from distant Ulster had given a slight tingle of anticipation but, for me, the championship only really began when it began close to home. The winners of this game – almost certainly Kildare – would be playing Dublin in the next round and this was a chance to see how good they would be. Even through the Valium, I could feel the tingle becoming a buzz.

   Kildare were, at the time, the perennial nearly men of football in the province of Leinster. Whoever was the dominant power in the province, Kildare were nearly as good – nearly, but not quite. In 1994 Kildare had been leading Dublin by one point almost as the referee put the whistle to his lips to blow up for full-time. Charlie Redmond had intervened with a heroic long-range point to drag Dublin into a replay, which they won easily.

Time and again this seemed to happen to Kildare. The team and its supporters were nicknamed 'the Lilywhites' on account of the all-white strip they wore, but we always suspected that when they began to wave their all-white flags it was more in surrender than in anticipation. No one doubted the ability of the team, but their attitude was regarded as suspect. Some suggested that the all-white jerseys hid a wide yellow streak that ran up their collective back. Louth, on the other hand, had a couple of good players and character in abundance, but, despite this, pundits in advance of the match were as sure Kildare would win this one as they had been sure Down would win a week earlier. The tension was palpable as the teams took to the field and I settled back to peer at the television screen through the fog of tranquillisers. On the pitch, the referee tossed in the ball, and four players hurled their bodies against each other, reaching, grasping for the ball. The season had begun.

Louth tore into Kildare before the Lilywhites knew the season had started. Louth were as lively as Kildare were lethargic, and before long the underdogs were two points in front. Then, slowly at first, the Kildare fightback began. Shaken from their slumber, Kildare began to exert the pressure that their superior ability demanded and by half-time were three points up. One could easily imagine their fans beginning to relax. In my mind's eye I could almost see them, shuffling their feet, gazing into the early evening summer sky and predicting the final score. Kildare by six points would be a fair result, I reckoned. I half wondered what was on the other channels.

But Louth weren't beaten yet. They started the second half like the first, ripping through Kildare with a ferocity that was not expected. Stefan White scored a great point and his team and his supporters found their spirits raised. Colin Kelly moved like quicksilver and Kildare seemed unable to tie him down. Now the pressure was on Kildare, and the old fears about their mental toughness began to hang in the air once more, undoubtedly haunting the fans but also, one suspected, the players. Kildare had possession of the ball, but not self-possession. Repeatedly they shot bad wides. Even on television you could hear their fans begin to turn on them, and the old questions about their temperament were now being asked.

There seemed plenty of time left and Louth were not taking advantage of Kildare's poor shooting. The game was still there for Kildare to take, if only they would, but, slowly, time slipped by. It was ten minutes since Kildare last scored. Then 15. Almost unbelievably, Louth had their noses in front, but there was still no need to panic. Kildare had spent the last six months training for this, three or four nights a week. In the dark nights of January and February these men had run and run till they threw up, and then they had run some more. They had kicked thousands of points and run hundreds of miles. They had been through rain, hail and burning pain over half a year to hone their bodies into teak, all for this moment. There were still ten minutes to go and now each player must have been asking himself, is this what all that was for? All the nights away from family, all the days spent aching in your muscles and in your gut. Five minutes to go. One minute. Now it was time to panic.

At the final whistle, Kildare had gone the last 25 minutes without scoring, and Louth were two-point winners, 0–13 to 0–11. They advanced to meet Dublin on 18 June. Kildare had trained from Christmas until the last week in May and their season had lasted just 70 minutes of play. Back in my mother's house, basking in the warm glow of the last of the Valium I had been prescribed, I picked up the remote control and flicked over to see what was on the other channels.

I remained bedridden for ten more days and then had a further few days of such limited mobility that I couldn't really leave the house. Then, bored beyond endurance with daytime television, I hobbled out of the house and back to work a week early. By that time, Down, Wexford, Kildare, Armagh, Offaly, Limerick, Waterford, Fermanagh, Sligo, Leitrim, Antrim, Longford and Westmeath had all been knocked out of the championship, and Dublin had not yet kicked a ball.

* * *

I was not the only one on the injured list that May. Ciaran Walsh had missed the 1994 All-Ireland final due to a hip injury. The team had felt his loss keenly and his absence had certainly contributed to the loss of the final. A few weeks before Dublin started their championship campaign, injury struck again: Walsh damaged his ankle ligaments and was ruled out of action for five to six weeks. In the 1994 final, Dublin had disastrously experimented by playing half-back Paul Curran in Ciaran Walsh's corner-back position. Curran was an excellent footballer but was not a specialist corner-back and had been quickly swamped when played out of position. That error could not be repeated. Luckily there were a couple of new, young players who had been brought into the senior team over the winter who were showing well in training. Gradually one of them, Keith Galvin, began to emerge as Walsh's likely replacement.

Many young players get caught in the headlights for a while when first called into the senior team. The thought of playing alongside the heroes they had previously watched from the terraces is overpowering for some. Like Jason Sherlock, Galvin was coming straight out of the previous year's underage team and, again like Sherlock, he played with an irrepressible confidence and did not seem at all fazed to be playing with the seniors. By inclination and talents, however, he was more an outfield player than a corner-back, and playing someone of his inexperience and inclination in the full-back line was a risk that would have to be constantly monitored. Meanwhile, Walsh began the slow process of trying to regain fitness. Eventually he was able to run on the ankle but only in straight lines. On Tuesdays, Thursdays and Saturdays, while his teammates twisted and turned through practice matches and training drills, Ciaran found himself in isolation, running laps of the pitch. On Mondays and Wednesdays he travelled to a pub owned by Fran Ryder, one of the management team, and ran yet more miles on a treadmill in the office there. There was no way he was going to be fit for Dublin's first game of the season but he could only hope that they would have a second and that he would be fit – and selected – for that.

Keith Barr too was carrying an injury into the season, although he was some weeks more advanced in his healing than Walsh. Keith knew – as did everyone – that every player's career begins with someone else getting injured or dropped. Now that he had the jersey he was determined to be selfish, to do everything he could to hang onto it. This drove him into training and into recovery. When the Louth game came around, he knew he would not be 100 per cent fit, but he would be ready.

* * *

The first match of the championship is always a potential problem, particularly when the opposition already have a game behind them. Although a team would have been training for six months, there is no fitness like match fitness and no whetstone that sharpens the reflexes and the mind like a tough championship match. In sports where the championship is organised in a league format, a team can often afford to take their time to find their feet and their rhythm. But, in the mid-1990s, the Gaelic football championship was organised strictly on a knockout basis. If you did not hit the ground running, your season was over after one game. On 18 June, Dublin would face Louth, who had already come through a tough and close encounter with Kildare. Dublin, on the other hand, had not played a game in three months. As banana skins go, Dublin's first match had the look of an oil slick. All this was in the mind as I scanned the papers for news the week before that opening match.

Normally, when reading the paper, I start on the front page and flick through from there, picking up pace as I go, until I reach the columnists' page. This gets a bit more attention before I go on to the 'Letters to the Editor' page. I scan through these (Nutter. Nutter. Absolute Nutter. Has he had a letter in before? Name looks familiar, not sure. Nutter, anyway. That one's good. Oh, another Nutter). From there, I bypass the business section and move on to the sports.

The week before a championship game, however, I start with the sports. Monday's paper is generally full of the previous day's results and reports. There would be nothing about next week's matches just yet, since the papers still had to pick over the entrails of the last lot of games. Leitrim were gone, their reign as champions in the west lasting only a year. I hadn't expected that. Leitrim had waited 67 years to win a Connacht title and then lost it on their first defence. The champions in Ulster and Connacht were both now gone. Was this a bad year to be a reigning provincial champion? Did that imply bad news for Dublin? Or was it simply that all the big guns were being taken out, easing Dublin's path to glory? Every article was scanned for what it said about other teams and for what it might mean to us.

Tuesday was still largely taken up with the previous weekend's games. After the initial flood of description and report, Tuesday was the time to analyse in a bit more depth and provide some mature reflection on the events of the weekend. The papers were still full of Leitrim being knocked out. Poor old Leitrim! There was not much to get excited about in Leitrim. It was the emigration capital of the island, with no real attractions except for the road to Dublin. Even in football terms they had been the poor relations of the poor man's province until the previous year, when the team had caught everyone unawares and won the Connacht title. In 1995, determined not to get caught again, entire villages had returned home from Dublin and beyond to see their first title defence in seven decades. They had been hot favourites going into the game and were still in front as normal time ended, but two points in injury time gave Galway victory by a single point. Long into the night in Carrick-on-Shannon post-mortems had raged, the paper said, but always tinged with local pride and undiminished enthusiasm for their county. 'That's nice,' I thought to myself. 'You wouldn't get it in Dublin. The Dubs would be too busy cursing their own forwards and calling for managerial resignations. Jesus, Leitrim people are the heart's blood of the Gaelic Athletic Association (GAA), what it's all really about. Local pride, representing your county, taking part. Great stuff. Now, fuck 'em. Bring on the Dubs!'

By Wednesday the papers were no longer dealing with the previous weekend but it was still too far away to be writing about the next Sunday. Thursday could be another slow day, although the teams would usually have been announced by Wednesday or Thursday and would be in the papers. You needed to scan carefully though, because sometimes team news was buried at the bottom of some other article. I took a look at the Dublin team sheet and got a tightening feeling in the pit of the stomach. Ciaran Walsh was out, replaced by Keith Galvin. I knew nothing of Galvin but knew that the loss of Walsh in the previous year's final had been costly for Dublin. Heading into the new season with some kid in the full-back line did not fill me with confidence. The problems were worse in the forwards. After the previous few years the general consensus was that Dublin needed a few new faces in the forward line, but there was nothing. Sean Cahill had been a sub the previous year, now he was a starter. Vinnie Murphy had been in and out of the team for the previous seven years. He was not a bad forward but had a tendency to wander into midfield in search of the ball and never really seemed to connect with his teammates. Paul Clarke had been in and out for years as well and seemed to have been tried in every position except in goal. Charlie Redmond, Mick Galvin and Dessie Farrell were all familiar names on the team sheet and I would not have changed any of them, but I had thought there might be some space for young Jason Sherlock. It seemed obvious that his commitment to professional soccer had impacted on his capacity to get to training, effectively making it hard for the management to select him. Overall, the vintage of 1995 looked a lot like the vintage of 1994, and that had ended, literally, in tears. The pit of my stomach tightened a little more.

Friday drifted past and brought some odd news. According to the paper, Ireland was doing well economically and seemed set to do better than other European countries. Economic confidence was high, inflation was low, construction was starting to do well and house prices were rising quickly. It didn't sound at all like any country that I would have recognised as Ireland. We talked about it over lunch in work and concluded that it would not last. There seemed to be no rumours in the paper as to how things were going in the Dublin squad and so I was left to speculate. Certainly Dublin should be too strong for Louth, I thought, but what if the Dubs were rusty and Louth were sharp? There was, I felt, too much experience in Dublin to get caught on a banana skin like Louth, but what if it was not experience, just age? By Friday evening the pit of my stomach was clenched as tight as the Gordian knot. 'Dublin could have gone out in the first round last year,' I told a bunch of largely uninterested people in the pub that evening. 'They should have, really. Kildare had Dublin beaten and any other team would have put us away. The season could have been over then and there. And Louth beat Kildare. In a tough, close game. Colin Kelly scored seven points against Kildare. Maybe he won't do that again, but I don't like this at all, not one little bit.' I couldn't wait for it to get started. I couldn't wait for Sunday.

* * *

If the fans had a sense of fear in advance of the game, so too did the players. Although pundits would have tended to dismiss Louth's chances against the Dubs, the management team believed that, in order to have an edge, the team needed to have a healthy degree of fear about the opposition. The players regarded Louth as a physical side and knew that they had posed problems for Dublin in league encounters and in challenge matches. For the players, the match came down to an individual battle with their marker; each one needed to win their own struggle first and foremost. Dessie Farrell found himself focusing on Stephen Melia, his direct opponent. Dessie had earlier approached the management team and had made a forceful case to be moved out of the full-forward line and into the half-forwards. Although he was named as starting in the full-forwards, it had been agreed that he would switch into a more outfield position and, having made such a strong case, he now had the added pressure of having to prove that the decision was the correct one. Bit by bit, it all added to the pressure of the game to come.

* * *

Although my back injury had healed sufficiently to allow me to be back at work in the week before Dublin's match against Louth, I was not yet fit enough to travel as far as Navan in County Meath, where the match was scheduled to be played. Consequently I was going to have to watch it on television. Although I would have loved to be at the game, I was well used to watching televised sports. When I was growing up, my parents had shown little interest in sport. My father had taken my brother to one or two soccer matches, but had never, as far as I could tell, set foot inside a Gaelic football ground. As a consequence, in the decade up to the early 1990s, most of my exposure to high-class sport had come through the cathode ray tube in the corner of the living room.

Not that there actually was much sport on the television when I was growing up, if truth be told. As a kid, I knew football and hurling happened, in part because it was the only thing on the radio on the occasions when the whole family was bundled into the car for a summer Sunday drive, and in part because, when I was ten years old, a youthful and enthusiastic teacher who was newly escaped from the wilds of Mayo and set loose on a bunch of Dublin kids, trained a team from amongst my classmates and brought them all the way to a Dublin schools' football final played in Croke Park. But I had never really seen proper grown-up Gaelic football because, into the '70s, only three football matches were broadcast live per year: the All-Ireland championship final and the two All-Ireland semi-finals. In the '70s we all knew the names of the great Dublin players, but most of my friends and I could not have picked them out of a police identity parade. Although we were the first generation in which almost every house had a television, our lack of exposure to televised football meant we were little different than the generation before us. In rural west Tipperary, not far from the county boundary with Limerick, Paddy Russell – who would, in 1995, referee the All-Ireland final – grew up in the 1960s in what were still the last days of the radio age. Few people in his area had a television and he remembers walking to a spot known as the crossroads where there was a house that had a television, in order to be able to see a match. As he walked up the road, he met other people all heading in the same direction, as the neighbourhood converged on one house to see the game. Later, in the early '70s, his Gaelic football team won a local championship and, as a prize, were sent to the All-Ireland football final where they saw Offaly win the title. Travelling up for the match, he and his teammates barely knew what the leading championship players looked like because they had hardly ever seen them. Even those who had seen players on television found that the reception was so grainy that it hardly merited watching.

At the time, no one in Ireland seemed really aware of the power of television to generate sporting heroes. In fact, many GAA people were more worried that showing matches on television for free would make the prospect of travelling a whole day to see a game less appealing (similar concerns had been voiced by US baseball team owners in the 1940s over the radio broadcasting of games). What they apparently didn't realise was that the problem was that they were showing too few matches, not too many: only by showing enough live games to generate a critical mass of interest would television have a positive impact on gate receipts. This realisation was, however, still far in the future. Indeed, the need for even limited television coverage only really became apparent to many GAA people when live soccer began to grow in popularity through television.

Throughout the 1970s, televised soccer or Gaelic football was still mostly based on highlights shows. Live matches in either code were a rarity but soccer was the more prominent of the two, and live matches sometimes became a big event. In our house, the English soccer FA Cup final was one such event – one of the few times each year that we were allowed to eat our dinner in front of the television. A table was set up in the sitting room and someone went out for chips while the rest of us buttered slices of white bread and made a big pot of tea. By the time the chips had been carried back from the chip shop they were nearly cold and had to be heated up under the grill but the whole thing had been timed to perfection and we sat down to eat just as the teams paraded out onto the Wembley stadium turf for the build-up to the game. I was nine years old when the 1981 Cup final between Spurs and Manchester City went to a replay. That was the year that Spurs' Argentinian Ricardo Villa twisted and turned his way through what seemed like the entire Manchester City team on his way to scoring what some still regard as one of the greatest ever goals in soccer. We talked about it for weeks and the kids who were better soccer players than me spent the following year slaloming their way through the duffel-coated crowds in the lunchtime schoolyard before slamming the ball against the gate that doubled as a goal and whirling away with their hands aloft, crying out their own commentary: 'Ricky Villa! Still Villa! He's still going! Gooaaaaalll!'

In the US they say that people who were alive at the time will always remember where they were when they heard that

John F. Kennedy had been shot. In a similar vein, I know exactly where I was when Ireland scored against England in the 1988 European Championship. I was 16 years of age, and, as a gangly and moderately clumsy teenager, I had found that team sports only made me feel bad about myself, and so I tried my best to ignore them. This did not simply apply to playing sports but also extended to watching them. I watched televised soccer the odd time, but would not go out of my way to see a soccer match if it was on – 90 minutes plus stoppages just seemed too long to sit in front of the television watching a game in which no one scored. I knew that Ireland were playing England that day (my brother had gone to Germany to follow the Irish team), but I, like many others, wasn't that pushed. The European Championship in 1988 was the first major international soccer tournament that Ireland had ever qualified for. For long-standing supporters of Irish soccer, this was an event of huge significance, a massive affirmation. Most of the country, however, was more sceptical and many people said, condescendingly, how well the team had done to get that far. Despite the undoubted talent of some of its members, the Irish national soccer team had, for a long time, been quite awful. Between 1980 and 1985 the team had played 40 games and had lost twice as many as they had won. Although the new manager, Englishman Jack Charlton, had brought some respectability to the side, most people feared that they could suffer badly at the hands of Europe's elite teams.

I was working in my local pub that afternoon, cleaning the place up during the lunchtime closing that was then a feature of Irish Sundays. At the precise moment that Ray Houghton's header looped into the corner of the English net, I was behind the bar, drying ashtrays as they came out of the dishwasher and grumbling about the fact that two of the barmen were watching the television and not doing any work. One of the barmen watching the television screamed, and, with incredulous glee, the two began to dance and scamper around the empty pub. I leapt over the bar as the whole staff descended on the television set to see the goal replayed and we were rooted to the spot as they replayed it again and again. It was more pinball than football in reality, as the ball ricocheted around the English box before looping into the net, but madly, and almost accidentally, the Irish team were in front. The television drew me towards it, and I suddenly found myself caring about the dizzy and unlikely drama being played out before me. When we believed that the Irish team had no chance, many of us had subconsciously decided not to pay any heed, but now it appeared as if Ireland might actually defeat the old enemy. Generations of dead patriots were recalled as the glimmer of possible victory gave us a sudden licence to care. I flinched and shouted like the rest, as all the staff gathered around the television and the pub remained half cleaned around us. Now that I was emotionally involved, 90 minutes passed in the flicker of an eye. When it was over, and Ireland had won, I was elated. The barmen, who had been watching from the outset, eyed new converts like me with sarcastic amusement but I didn't care. I was hooked. Soccer suddenly took on new meaning. I would never play for Ireland, I knew, but, as the rush of emotion coursed through my veins like some potent drug, I immediately recognised the addictive buzz of being a supporter.

I was not the only one to jump on the bandwagon. Flags began to appear throughout the length and breadth of the land and market traders in Dublin's Moore Street opened up a profitable new line of business by selling souvenir T-shirts by the truckload. I watched in a friend's house as the team drew their next game against the Soviet Union, and suddenly they looked like genuine contenders. By the time their third match took place, the country had been gripped with soccer fever. They lost the game 1–0 to a Dutch goal that probably should have been disallowed but in defeat they had represented us bravely and admirably, and the country fell in love with our new sporting heroes. The great Dutch team of Ruud Gullit, Frank Rijkaard and Marco van

Basten showed how good Ireland really were when they went on to win the tournament, beating the Soviet Union in the final.

Two years later the Irish national team qualified for the World Cup tournament being held in Italy. Once more, their opening game was against England and this time the country was not going to be caught unawares, as had happened in 1988. The match kicked off on an early summer evening on the same day that I finished my first year university exams, and the students' bar – like every other pub in the country – was full and decked out in the colours of the national flag. It hardly mattered that many people who were now vociferous supporters of the national team hardly knew the rules of the game or that few of us had ever set foot inside the ground of a League of Ireland soccer club. When the journalist and former Irish soccer international Eamon Dunphy dared to question the tactics that Charlton was imposing upon the team, the country rose in the spontaneous fury of a lynch mob and Dunphy was castigated for his failure to jettison analysis and follow the national mood. By the time we – the team had by now stopped being 'they' and had become 'we' – beat Romania and qualified to play Italy in Rome, many shops and businesses had taken to closing during matches and the entire country seemed enthralled in a delirious holiday romance with ourselves. Grown men fought back tears as the evening news broadcast pictures of the Irish team's audience with the Pope and as he wished us good luck. By the time we took to the field in Rome on a warm summer night, the tears were no longer being fought back and men and women cried with abandon and pride.

Afterwards, we said that it was the greatest game the Irish team had ever played. The team tore into the home side with delicious abandon. In pubs at home, the length of the country, we ran every inch with our team. I was, once more, working behind the bar of my local pub and I remember how the anguish and hope of the game crashed through the room in waves that night. We put the Italians under pressure and never gave them an inch in which to perform their magic. But the Italians too were magnificent. Toto Schillaci scored and we were 1–0 down, but our team never gave up. We scooped pints across the bar as fast as our arms could manage and then we sang and clapped and cheered along with the customers and felt our hearts fill with pride and love. When the final whistle sounded, Ireland were out, but, on both sides of the bar, we put down our glasses and stood and clapped in a wordless but tearful ovation to the boys in green.

It is hard now to make sense of how we felt in those crazy weeks of the early summer of 1990. Ireland in the late 1980s was a devastated country. The economic depression that had affected much of the world in the 1980s hit Ireland like a plague. Unemployment began to spiral ever upwards until by 1987 one man in six was unemployed and over half of those had been out of work for more than a year. Parts of Dublin city centre were populated with decaying, dilapidated buildings jutting like broken teeth along the riverside. One senior minister encouraged young people to emigrate, telling us that 'we can't all live on a small island'. Many took his advice: between 1981 and 1990, 358,000 Irish people left to make a life for themselves in other countries.

The progress of the Irish soccer team at the end of the 1980s and into the early 1990s gave Irish people a source of pride when we had nothing else to be proud about. They won nothing, but that too was all right, because Irish heroes were not meant to win. Daniel O'Connell was a national icon who had the main streets of Dublin and Limerick named after him, although he died without achieving his aim of repeal of the Act of Union. We had named streets after Charles Stuart Parnell too, even though he had also failed to achieve Home Rule before his career and his life were ended prematurely. All of our revolutionary heroes, from Wolfe Tone in 1798 to Padraig Pearse and James Connolly in 1916, had been spectacular failures and in their failure we had made them heroes because Ireland always carved its icons from men who had come close and failed. Success was not expected, but tragic and glorious failure was lauded: 'As someone said after John Kennedy was shot, there is no point in being Irish if you don't realise that your heart is going to be broken eventually,' wrote Matthew Engel in an English newspaper, and he was right. Our soccer team had played their part. From the so-close-but-yet-so-far-away losing goal against the Dutch in 1988 to their epic stand against the Italians in Rome in 1990, all their battles had ultimately been lost and all had been glorious.

The success of the Irish national soccer team in qualifying for the European Championship in 1988 and for the World Cup in 1990 and 1994 – all of which were watched on television – contributed to the growing enthusiasm for televised soccer. In 1992 the English Premier League was established and Sky television began to provide wall-to-wall live televised soccer. The mass marketing that Sky brought to English soccer helped to increase its market in Ireland, and sport and television became enmeshed as never before. Monday night in the pub became a regular fixture for the lads and me, and televised sport began to ratchet up its presence in our lives.

At the time, soccer was the dominant televised sport. The GAA were still nervous about television, but, since the soccer season ended in the summer, just as the football championship season was commencing, there was no clash and no worry. The European Championship and World Cup in 1988 and 1990 changed that. For the first time, soccer and Gaelic football began to clash. Initially at least, it was Gaelic games that came out the worst and the championship season of 1990 passed much of the country by as we gazed in rapture at the exploits of our soccer team in Italy on television.

In a sense, the comparative weakness of Gaelic games in comparison with international soccer was part of a bigger problem for the GAA. The soccer team managed by Jack Charlton and supported by growing legions of followers – Jack's army – redefined Ireland. The GAA had always understood itself as part of the great national project of defining Irish identity, but the identity that project sought to forge was one that many found unappealing. Irish nationalists had envisaged Ireland as Catholic, rural, happily poor and Gaelic, but by the 1990s that vision was one which many looked on with, at best, humorous disbelief; at worst, repulsion. For those of us from Dublin, the idea that Ireland should be understood as rural had long given rise to a problem of identity. In school, we recited Irish language lessons about 'a day on the bog', but never a day on the concrete. We learned about birds and badgers that we never saw and read poems which spoke of gaps in hedges and lost cattle. Dublin folk were of Ireland but, somehow, we didn't belong. But soccer, unlike Gaelic football, had always been associated with Dublin. Now the nation wanted it, and if they wanted it, they would have to take us too. When Roddy Doyle, Dublin's poet laureate, described the feeling in 1990 when Ireland played Italy in the World Cup, he wrote, 'It was one of the greatest times of my life, when I loved being from Dublin and I loved being Irish.' Soccer wasn't just about being from Ireland. It was about being from Dublin too.

The Irish soccer team's exploits on the European and world stage created an opportunity for Irish people to relate sport to a new type of national identity, one that was not associated in their minds with an older nationalism. The soccer team was managed by an Englishman, and had players from black, Asian, Italian and Scottish backgrounds. It was a team that represented the Ireland we were becoming. In a sense, the tables had been turned by the soccer fans. For much of the life of the state, they had been in an ambiguous position: nationalists who supported a 'foreign' game. Now it was the GAA fan who was in an ambiguous position, and none more ambiguous than the Dublin GAA fan. To the rest of the country, we were always Dubs, but to others in Dublin, we were regarded as countrified. For me this had all come to a head the previous year on a strange and surreal Saturday, 18 June 1994. That was the day Ireland opened the 1994 World Cup by playing

Italy in Giants Stadium, New Jersey. In the US, it was the day that O.J. Simpson set off in his white Bronco van on a bizarre slow-motion car chase that was broadcast live around the world and ended with his arrest for murder. Nearer to home, many pubs in Dublin were closed due to a strike that warm summer's day and the Dubs were opening the 1994 campaign with a match against Kildare.

The country was adorned with green, white and orange flags that day and Dublin was abuzz with talk of the match against the Italians that evening. The game was dubbed as the battle of New York's immigrants – Italians against Irish – and we wondered who would bring the bigger crowd. We wondered too if we might savour delicious revenge for our defeat at their hands four years earlier. The Italians were notoriously slow starters in this sort of tournament, so we knew we had a chance. The country was abuzz. But first the Dubs.

For me there was no clash between the two games, and I set off early in the afternoon to Hill 16, the spiritual home of the Dub. As I and thousands of other Dubs strode through the sunlit streets to Croke Park, we passed by the working-class housing estates and flat complexes that surround the stadium. Suddenly, from the balconies above, a child's voice rang out: 'Yez fucking rednecks!' I looked around for a minute to see where the Kildare fans were he was abusing, but there were none in sight. 'Where's yer fuckin' wellies, yez bogmen, yez,' he called again. I looked up.

He was looking straight at me.

Being branded a bogman by one of my own hurt, but there was no time to be discussing identity politics with him, so I told him to fuck off and headed for the Hill. Even if I had stopped to try to resolve the issue, there would have been no resolution to be had because it is in the nature of identities to shift and change and to be the subject of conflict. In the years that followed, the place of the Irish soccer team in our self-imagination would change too. We didn't know it at the time but by 1994 the Irish soccer team had already passed their peak and were in decline. The following year, in May and early June of 1995, while I was laid out with a slipped disc and Ciaran Walsh was testing the strength in his ankle, they blew their chance of qualifying for the European Championship finals when, in the space of a single week, they failed to beat Liechtenstein – a state little bigger than an Irish town – and then lost to Austria. The manager was gone by the end of the year. At the time, though, we thought the soccer bandwagon would roll on forever and that they were simply gearing up for another championship.

That meant that Gaelic football and hurling were under serious pressure to maintain their market share in the nation's imagination. Blackburn Rovers had, just two weeks previously, won English soccer's Premier League title on the last day of the season in a roller-coaster match which had provided a dramatic finale to an action-packed season (which had earlier seen Manchester United's Eric Cantona suspended for his spectacular and bizarre karate-kick lunge into the crowd at a thuggish 'fan' who had been shouting racist abuse at him). Rugby too was making an impact on people's consciousness as never before in 1995. The Irish team had recently turned professional and early that summer they were competing in the rugby World Cup in South Africa against New Zealand and the awesome Jonah Lomu. Their preparations for the World Cup and the advance publicity for the event itself had consumed much of the late spring/early summer media coverage – coverage that would normally have been taken up with hurling or Gaelic football. Gaelic football had weathered the initial challenge well and the saga of Dublin against Meath in 1991 had won back to the GAA many fans that had slipped away during the soccer championships of 1988 and 1990. The epic Dublin and Meath clashes also led to an increase in the number of televised matches but they were still a far from regular occurrence. By 1995, however, the televising of Gaelic games had become a crucial issue for the GAA.

This made it all the more bizarre that the televising of the Down match on the opening day of the season had been cancelled at the last minute due to a row between RTÉ and the GAA. By the Tuesday of the following week, tentative signs of reconciliation between the two organisations began to be seen. Their cautious courtship continued for much of the following week. The GAA were by now anxious to have televised live coverage of games but did not want televised Gaelic games to clash with non-televised games in case this would have an impact on attendances. This meant that games that were to be shown live would have to be staged at sometime other than a Sunday mid-afternoon.

While this may look, at first glance, like a small matter of shuffling the fixture list, this issue was to become a bone of major contention. For many people, the timetable for the Sunday of a championship match was a fixed matter of ritual that had almost religious significance. On a match Sunday they woke up in the morning with an excited giddiness in their stomach at a specified time, ate their fried breakfast at a specified time, went to Mass at a specified time and were in the specified pub for the specified number of pints before heading into the game at the specified time. Changing this timetable was no small matter. The ritual had been developed over many years and with much trial and error to ensure that just the right amount of food and drink was consumed at just the right pace to ensure that the supporter was in good form for the match. Changing the ritual could mean too little time in the pub, which would mean that you weren't sufficiently lubricated for the game. Worse still, it could mean too long in the pub, which might mean having to leave your space to take a piss during the game – a course of action which was manfully avoided by all who had seen the inside of the toilets in any football ground in the country. All things considered, the idea of a game starting at any time other than 3.15 on a Sunday afternoon was not something to be taken lightly. Just as the Pope had called a Vatican Council to change the ritual of the Mass, many football fans were of the opinion that at least as august a body should be required to think over the ritual of a championship Sunday before any changes could be contemplated.

The GAA were, however, adamant that television coverage of live games could not clash with other games. Just as 30 years earlier, there was a failure to realise that the more live games there were, the greater would be the interest generated. Early in the week, cautiously optimistic signals began to be generated from the negotiations, and word came out that the clash between Louth and Kildare would be televised live at the very unusual time of 6.15 on Sunday evening. Much grumbling and discussion ensued about how the 'genuine supporter' was going to be led on a merry dance all to suit the needs of the lily-livered television-watching types who wouldn't brave the treacherous roads and weather conditions to see a match. But, when Louth's shock victory over Kildare took place the following Sunday, the sky did not fall in on the supporter and we got our first live televised Gaelic football match of the year.

As it turned out, Louth's second game that year — their clash with Dublin — was also televised. This was a matter of great delight to me since I was not fit to travel to the game. I therefore made arrangements to watch it with some friends, a couple of brothers from Louth. This could, I knew, be something of a dangerous strategy: if the match went badly for the Dubs I could expect some serious slagging. On the other hand, if the Dubs did give Louth a hiding then I would be the one to rub it in. I was worried about the match but it was still worth the risk and so, at 6.15 that Sunday evening, I found myself crouched on the edge of the sofa in front of their television, wound as tightly as a broken watch and flanked on either side by Louth men. All the talk and supposition had come to an end. This was to be the moment of truth.

Dublin were like a greyhound, ready to erupt from the traps once the door was sprung. Inside the first minute they won a free, which Charlie sent over the bar. Back on the sofa I inched forward, fist clenched, punching the air, a silent grimace on my face. Dublin seemed too physically strong for their opponents, muscling them off the ball and winning a lot of good possession. The ball was worked around for another score and Dublin were two points clear. Then a third score came, this time from Paul Clarke. Ten minutes were gone in the match and the Dubs were in control.

All was not right, however. Vinnie Murphy had not got into the game and Sean Cahill looked nervous and shot a couple of bad wides. For all their dominance, Dublin were only three points up. Then two, as Colin Kelly hit back with a point from a free. Immediately, Charlie Redmond responded with a free of his own, the perfect response. Then Dublin started to ease away from Louth. Cahill was called ashore: in his first championship start he had disintegrated into a ball of nerves. He was replaced by young Sherlock, and almost immediately Jason had the ball in his hands and was scampering up the right wing at the Louth defence. His marker was twice his size but Sherlock somehow held him off before running into the Louth cover. There were two men around him now, and although he was only metres from goal, he was going nowhere. He spotted a teammate outside him and his slick hand pass deceived the two defenders who now set off chasing the ball, leaving Sherlock in the clear once more. The ball was moved quickly through two Dublin players' hands and suddenly it was back with Sherlock in front of goal. He shaped as if to shoot, but before he could, the Louth defence descended upon him like an avalanche. The referee blew the whistle and awarded the penalty.

Back in Dublin, Ken, one of my friends from Louth, breathed an exaggerated and dramatic sigh of relief. 'Dublin penalty! Phew. That's all right then. No worries about a score here,' he said.

'Ha fucking ha. It's good to still be able to laugh when your side is six points down and being beaten like a mangy dog.'

Still, deep inside me a little voice was saying that the last thing Dublin needed now was a penalty. If it went in, that was great – the rest of the game would be like shooting fish in a barrel. If not, it was the sort of thing that could change the direction of a match. I inched forward on the sofa and chewed on the side of a fingernail. Come on, Dubs!

On the field in Navan, Paul Clarke stood up to take the penalty. He faced the goalkeeper, full of confidence, and then hammered the ball low and to the keeper's right. It was a well-taken penalty but the keeper got down and somehow got his body behind it. Either side of me, Fergus and Ken jumped to their feet, while on the field the ball squirted around before the referee blew his whistle again and awarded a free out to Louth. Dublin got back up and scored another point, but Louth now had renewed confidence. The penalty save had lifted them. Still, they were seven points down as half-time approached. They were a long way off yet.

There seemed to be no danger. The ball was played into the Louth half-forward line but there were two Dublin players there. Although there was no danger, they wrestled their man rather than tackling him. The referee blew up for a free to Louth. Another point on the way, it seemed, but the Louth player had a different idea. Looking up, he spotted that Cathal O'Hanlon had lost Keith Barr, his marker, and was drifting in towards goal. The ball was lofted over the heads of retreating Dublin players and, too late, they realised what was unfolding. John O'Leary started to come off his goal line, then hesitated, knowing he would not get to the ball first. O'Hanlon jumped unopposed and batted the ball towards goal with two fists. O'Leary leapt despairingly, agonisingly getting his fingertips to the ball, but it was beyond him. The ball dropped into the net. Louth were back in this game. Shit.

But the Dubs knuckled down and drove back into Louth. Within five minutes they had posted another three points, the last of which was scored by Sherlock after he had been flattened a second time. Charlie Redmond later recalled, 'Not long after he came on he got a free. The Louth lads were having a go at Jason, targeting him. You can't blame them really, they were just trying to get an advantage. I threw the ball to him and said, "Best way you can answer them is to put the ball over the bar." I thought that giving him the easy score would settle him, but I realised he was looking very nervous. He said, "What?" and I said, "Just knock the fucking thing over," but I was thinking, "Jesus Christ, am I doing the right thing here?" I looked at the sideline and Pat O'Neill had his hands on his hips and was looking at me as if to say "What the fuck is going on here?" Thankfully he put it over and I think it settled him. He had a decent game after that. That's one of the things we learned about Jason as we went on: Jason was a different player then to the player he is now. In 1995, he couldn't kick the ball 25 yards! It was only later I realised that when I gave him that 14-yard free, that was probably his full distance. He gave us a special dimension though, close to goal.'

The three quick points seemed to have closed the door on Louth and at half-time it looked like their fire had been almost extinguished: Dublin 0–11, Louth 1–1 (four points). Seven points up at half-time. This game should be over.

Back in Dublin, I sat back a bit on the sofa, breathing something of a satisfied sigh. Now was the time to pick over the first half and try to divine from it the omens for the second. There was a problem, however. When you watch a game on television you miss most of what is going on. You cannot see players running off the ball, switching positions or working hard to get into position away from the camera. You can see the team winning possession or scoring points but often it is hard to tell why. Half-time comes and you want to pick over the game and read what is going right and what is not but you are missing much of the information you need to come to a judgement. It is as if you are getting to read only every fourth page in an Agatha Christie novel and yet still have to figure out who the murderer is.

On one hand the scoreline said it all. Dublin had scored 11 times, Louth twice. Dublin's defence was clearly doing well. Dermot Deasy at centre-back had Colin Kelly in his pocket. Kelly had scored more than half of Louth's points against Kildare but in the first half against Dublin he hadn't scored from play at all. I was struck with admiration for Dermot Deasy. At his age he wasn't too fast, but his vision and his reading of the game were remarkable. It was true that the defence had been caught napping a bit for the goal and that was a worry, but generally they had dominated their men. Given that Dublin's weaknesses were supposed to be up front, 11 points in half a game looked like a hell of a return. That would be good enough to win some games. At the same time, some of them were misfiring. Vinnie Murphy hadn't really got into the game but Sherlock had looked threatening since he had come on. He seemed able to unsettle defenders and had the vision to pick out players around him. Fergus handed me a cup of black coffee strong enough to blind a horse and I asked him what he thought. 'Louth are shite,' he said. 'True enough,' I thought to myself. I hadn't actually considered that as an explanation.

But, if Louth were shite, no one seemed to have told them. They came blazing out for the second half and within five minutes of the restart had chalked up as many scores as they did in the whole of the first half. It was now 0–11 to 1–3, with Dublin still ahead by five points. Ger Canning, the match commentator on the television, was advising viewers that Dublin hadn't yet found their rhythm in this second half, and, as if to illustrate the point, a Dublin player failed to reach a lofted ball from the sideline and it dropped into the chest of Louth's danger man, Stefan White. He was still 25 metres out with his back to goal and three defenders were between him and the net, so there seemed no danger.

Then Keith Barr, White's marker, slipped, giving him a few vital metres. White dropped his shoulder and swung to his right as the corner-forward darted across his path, drawing defenders to him. Distracted by the crossing player, the blue shirts parted in front of White like the Red Sea opening before Moses. Like a flash, he was through on goal and slipped the ball beneath the advancing John O'Leary and into the bottom corner of the net. Goal! Shit! There were now just two points between the teams and a remarkable comeback was almost complete. Twenty-five minutes to go. Game on.

After a goal, the next point is always crucial. If Louth scored again then they would have hammered home the psychological advantage of the goal. If Dublin could hold them for a few minutes, however, they could steady their nerves and put some doubt back into Louth. On the sofa, my friends were jubilant, but I was just getting serious. 'Come on, Dubs,' I shouted at the television, oblivious to the fact that the players couldn't hear me. 'You're much better than this shower! Put them away, for fuck sake!' My friends might well have taken offence at being referred to as 'this shower' but I had forgotten they were there and forgotten where I was. All my attention was focused on the television screen.

Dublin were winning the ball again around the middle of the field and Dessie Farrell popped up with a score, his first. He had moved to centre half-forward now and was expertly orchestrating proceedings in front of him. Dublin scored again, another free from Charlie Redmond, and you sensed that the floodgates were about to open. Louth started to look ragged once more as the power and precision of the Dublin play drained their confidence and their resolve. Dublin were scoring at will now. Louth repeatedly found themselves giving away free-kicks in good positions and Charlie Redmond punished them every time. By the end of the 70 minutes he had scored nine points (eight from frees) and Dublin were eight-point winners on a

0–19 to 2–5 (11 points) scoreline. The Louth team who had played so well against Kildare were nowhere to be seen.

The following day, I would buy all the morning papers and carefully read the match reports in order to discern just whether or not Dublin were likely to be still playing a role in the championship in September. The forward line had looked well balanced when Dessie Farrell went to the half-forward position and used his vision and passing to distribute the ball. Dublin did score 19 times, a great score from a forward line that was supposed to be the team's weak link, and Dermot Deasy had been phenomenal at full-back, a man whose quickness of thought took years off of his legs. Keith Galvin had done very well in his first start in the corner-back position although his job had been made easier by the tendency of his marker to wander out towards midfield in search of the ball. On the other hand, Keith Barr, our irrepressible centre half-back enforcer and leader of the Dublin crazy gang, had been in part responsible for both of the goals. I hoped it was just one bad day at the office, because if his performances started to drop we were screwed.

All those questions, however, were for another day. The match night was reserved for baiting the friends who had been kind enough to offer me their hospitality for the game. I leaned back on the sofa, hands behind my head in as smug a posture as I could manage. 'Told you we should be putting away this sort of shower,' I said.

'Fuck off,' one, quite reasonably, replied.

* * *

On the same day that Dublin were playing Louth, their next-round opponents were also being decided in Portlaoise, where Laois were playing Carlow. On the face of it, it looked likely to be a cut and dried encounter. Laois were a good side who had fallen victim to geography. Had they been in any province other than Leinster they would certainly, at some time over the previous few decades, have won a provincial title. Trapped in Leinster behind Dublin, Meath and Offaly, however, they had not won a provincial title since 1946 and did not look like winning one anytime soon. Carlow, on the other hand, looked like one of the many sides who took to each season's championship with undiminished enthusiasm despite the fact that they had no chance whatsoever of winning a provincial or All-Ireland title. The two were near neighbours and that always brought a certain frisson to any game but it essentially seemed like a game that would mean a great deal to the supporters of each team and little to anyone else. Instead it turned into a game that sent shockwaves throughout the GAA for the rest of the season.

With only minutes to go and with nothing between the sides, a Laois player punted a ball towards the posts and everyone in the ground watched it drift wide. Everyone, that is, except the referee and the umpire beside the goal whose job it was to indicate when a score had taken place. After a consultation between the two, a point was awarded, much to the fury of the Carlow supporters who began to chant 'Cheat! Cheat! Cheat!' at the referee. Moments later things got worse when the referee ruled that Carlow had opted to take a free-kick quickly from the hand when the player insisted he had not heard the whistle and was simply playing on. Occurring late in the game, these two incidents were the difference between Carlow winning a famous victory over their near neighbours and great rivals and a one-point defeat. It was heartbreaking for the Carlow players and many slumped in tears at the final whistle, but it was also the same sort of honest refereeing mistake that happens every day at games throughout the country and the globe.

Television would, over the next few years, help to re-establish Gaelic games' centrality to the Irish sporting imagination. Starting by showing a live game every weekend and eventually moving to two or three live games every weekend, they would help to create a sense of carnival around Gaelic games which would increase attendances and gate receipts to the GAA. Newspapers would also join the pageant and the amount of Gaelic games coverage would increase exponentially in future years. But the GAA's dalliance with the media would come at a price. Everyone who made Gaelic football happen, from the players to the referees, were unpaid for their endeavours and took part solely because of their love of the game. Everyone, that is, except journalists and pundits, who were, in a sense, among the few to benefit monetarily from Gaelic games. In order for the media to pay wages they needed to sell advertising and this meant that games, no matter how indifferent the play, must be talked up as if they were the Battle of Stalingrad. When a genuine controversy did occur, the media whipped it up until it became the greatest scandal since the CIA helped the Mafia to shoot John F. Kennedy.

The day after Carlow played Laois, newspapers were bursting with accounts of what they called 'the point that never was' and they carried large pictures of the referee being given a police escort off the field as furious Carlow supporters sought to reach him. Some of the coverage was measured and reasonable but more of it was wild and inflammatory. It was television that proved crucial, however. The slow-motion replay of the Laois shot showed clearly that the ball had passed wide of the posts. The footage was played what seemed like a thousand times as if something different was somehow likely to transpire the next time it was played but each time the ball slid wide of the posts and television pundits wound up the controversy and heightened the pressure on the referee. According to the rules, the referee's decision was final and there was no facility for television evidence to be taken into account. Yet justice had clearly not been done to Carlow. The media campaign for justice for the Carlow 15 quickly gathered momentum.

In the end it was Laois who spared the GAA's blushes by offering a replay to Carlow. Everyone was happy, except, one presumed, the referee who had participated in the game for no reward other than the love of the game and who, for his troubles, had been made a national whipping boy because he made a simple, honest mistake and had been found out by television pundits who, unlike him, had no responsibility for the game, but did have the benefit of television replays. It marked a new departure for the GAA, and was an early signal of what the increased media coverage might mean. Although no one could have known it at the time, it would not be the last time that season that the media's capacity for endless television replays would enable them to turn a contested refereeing decision into a national witch-hunt.

Three

Blue Spanish Sky

THE WEEKS AFTER DUBLIN'S first-round game with Louth in 1995 were scorching. Temperatures rose to almost 30 degrees centigrade (86 degrees Fahrenheit) in the shade, with some parts of Ireland experiencing the same temperatures as the Spanish tourist resorts of Mallorca and Benidorm. Dublin was awash with exposed skin quickly turning from bluish-white to pink, then lobster red, as all advice from the National Safety Council was swept aside in the headlong rush to sun worship. Grassy stretches in St Stephen's Green and Trinity College became littered with sprawled, semi-naked bodies soaking up all of the rays they could catch. The sun was here and there was no guarantee it would last beyond the weekend, so the Irish were determined to catch it while they could.

For the Dublin squad, training on balmy summer evenings seemed light years removed from the grinding slog in the darkness under biting rain that they had endured in late January and early February. On those winter nights the rain had fallen like iron rods, whipping every inch of exposed skin red raw and making it hard to catch your breath. In the warm, bright evenings of early summer, however, such nights were almost unimaginable and players now looked forward to jumping into the car after work and driving across the city to the training grounds in Santry, listening on the radio to the news or to one of the music stations, all of which seemed to be perpetually playing The Rembrandts' theme song from the sitcom *Friends*. Dublin football had, since the '70s, been based on the simple principle that no one would be fitter than the Dubs. Fran Ryder, who had played on the team of the '70s, was the member of the management team who took responsibility for fitness training and, by June, the side were fitter than any in the country and on their way to becoming one of the fittest units to ever play the game.

There were a number of injury concerns hanging over the team, however. Keith Barr's hamstring was not right and Dermot Deasy was also having trouble. Deasy played directly in front of John O'Leary in goal, and Barr played in front of him again. These two injury concerns meant that Dublin were weakened in the central spine of the team. More than that, Barr was an iconic figure for the team and the supporters, a larger-than-life character who anchored the team psychologically as well as physically. Deasy's injury meant that, of the three members of Dublin's full-back line, two were now doubtful due to injury.

The other injury worry was Ciaran Walsh. As the match against Laois approached, Walsh was still waiting for full fitness to return. Waiting was something he was good at. He had broken into the Dublin squad in the late '80s and found himself waiting for a place in the team behind Gerry Hargan, Dublin's All-Star defender. A lot of other players would have lost heart at continuing to turn out and train while someone else held the starting spot in the team but Walsh was younger than Hargan and had time on his side and so felt able to wait. He had made his way into the championship team in 1991, just in time to play his part in that year's great Dublin and Meath four-match epic, only to find himself substituted in the third match when Gerry Hargan made a triumphant return to the side. Hargan stuck around for one more season and, apart from an appearance as a substitute that year, Walsh was forced to wait through Dublin's run to the All-Ireland final in 1992 as well. All this time he was aware that, at any time, another player could arrive in the side and move into the reckoning for the starting spot ahead of him. Still, he waited.

In 1993, five years after first getting a run-out in the Dublin team, he finally nailed down his starting place in the team and had been ever present in the side up until injury had ruled him out of the All-Ireland final in 1994. When injury had again forced him to miss the first game of the 1995 season, he found himself waiting again. Although not fully fit as the second game of the season approached, he had felt that his experience and understanding of corner-back play would ensure a return to the team. The management, however, had felt that Keith Galvin had done nothing wrong in his first outing against Louth and that dropping him under the circumstances would be harsh. When the team was announced at training on the Tuesday before the match, Ciaran Walsh was told he would be starting on the bench. He was waiting once more.

* * *

The Friday before the match, I had arranged to meet a friend in a newly refurbished pub in Dublin city centre. The pub was one of a growing number of decent old hostelries that were renovating away all of their character and replacing it with chrome, glass and loud music in the hope of attracting younger people with disposable income. The ploy was apparently successful because the number of genuine old Dublin pubs seemed in terminal decline and, by the time I arrived on Friday evening, the place was jammed with people, many of whom had come straight from work hours earlier. I wandered around the pub for a few minutes looking for a free stool, then took it to join the bunch of people I was to meet. I knew only a couple of them well; the rest were friends of friends, some of whom I knew vaguely, some not at all. Two tables had been pushed together to facilitate the whole group and by the time I arrived there were already quite a few empty glasses on the table and conversation was in full tilt, so I ordered a drink and set about catching up. The conversation was loud, raucous and smutty and was flying when I felt a tap on my shoulder.

'Sorry,' said the young woman who was standing there, 'is this seat free?' She was pointing to an unoccupied seat beside me. I wasn't sure who it belonged to, but I gestured to her to sit down. I recognised her vaguely from somewhere. She was very good looking, my own age, slim with a delicate build and loose red hair that fell in what was undoubtedly a carefully sculpted look of carelessness around her face. We introduced ourselves to each other and talked for a minute or two about where we had previously seen each other. Then the conversation started to dry up and we both leaned forward to try and pick up the thread of the chat around the table. It had splintered into a number of different fragments by then, however, and, not being engaged in any of them, we started once more to talk to each other. I was extremely conscious of the fact that she was an attractive woman and, given half a chance, I would have liked to make a move on her, but first I had to overcome my tendency to turn into a geek and freak out in the company of a good-looking woman. The couple of quick pints had made me brave now and I started to try to turn on the charm. 'Don't overdo it, now,' I warned myself furiously. 'Remember: you are available but not desperate. That is what you are trying to communicate. Laugh at the jokes, don't cackle. Just take it easy.'

But my warning to myself seemed unnecessary. Suddenly, the conversation just started to flow. I downed my next pint a bit too swiftly, my nerves getting the better of me, but it seemed to lubricate my vocal cords and in a matter of minutes the conversation was roaring along and I could feel the connection. I told her this story, then that story, relaxing and just letting myself talk. Fifteen minutes in and I could definitely feel a spark. After 20, I was sure there was electricity between us. But, just before I moved on to phase two of my grand plan (making initial physical contact by putting my hand on her arm as I told a story), a horrific realisation started to dawn, and I asked her, 'Am I right in thinking that you haven't said a word in 20 minutes?'

She nodded.

There was silence. My heart crashed from my throat to my ankles when a second, even more horrific, realisation dawned. 'And is that because I have been talking about Gaelic football for the last 20 solid minutes?' I asked.

She nodded once again.

'You are bored out of your tree, aren't you?'

'Basically.'

'But why did you let me just rabbit on like that?' I asked. 'How come you didn't . . .' I searched for words, '. . . just get up and move?'

'The place is jammed,' she said with a shrug, then took a sip of her drink. 'There wasn't another free seat.' And then, as if in an afterthought, she added, 'And my feet are killing me.'

* * *

I couldn't wait for Dublin's second – and my first – championship match of the summer to come around. The season's first game was a chance to meet friends whom I did not see from one end of the year to another. Although the rest of the lads had already had one day out together against Louth, this was my chance to catch up with a gang of lads that I had not seen since the wet and ultimately heartbreaking day of the previous year's All-Ireland final. We were not close friends as a group, though some individuals within the group were close. Yet our common purpose gave us an easy familiarity which meant that we didn't need to know each other well or to think of picking up the phone to each other from September to June. We watched matches together. That was what made us a group. We sang together, slagged each other, hugged each other with furious joy when the occasion called for it, and leaned on each other's shoulders when we needed support. Watching matches together was enough.

We would slip into conversation easily, as if we had seen each other last only the previous week. The first conversation always began with someone saying, 'I can feel it. This is our year!' before giving rise to a meandering and pessimistic assessment of our chances to which everyone contributed. This then led on to the second required conversation: 'We need to get a flag this year, one of the enormous ones. A great big fuck-off-sized flag.' Each year began with these same two conversations, which always followed the same course. We were all pessimistic about the Dubs (so as not to bring bad luck upon ourselves by saying positive things), and the flag was never bought. Only after these two conversations did we slip into anything else like 'How are you?' or 'What have you been doing these last nine months?'

The sun was still shining on Sunday morning when we set off for Navan bright and early in two cars, three people per car. Although it should have taken only an hour or so to get there, we expected there to be substantial traffic on the road and figured it was best to arrive early rather than getting stuck on the way and miss the match. I had shaved my head completely two weeks previously under the influence of a hangover and had liked the look so much that I had continued to keep it shaved. This was the first time the lads had been treated to the sight of my glorious, gleaming, bone-white scalp, and there was a great deal of slagging about my new hairless style and also about my choice of headgear, a white panama hat of the type normally seen on cricket umpires. I had got the idea for the hat from a Yellow Pages advert on one of the British television channels at the time and had spent an entire Saturday searching Dublin high and low for it. Eventually I found one which was slightly too small and which therefore sat up too high on my head. The sales clerk assured me that this was the way panama hats were worn and, although I didn't believe him, I bought it anyway. I liked the eccentricity of it. I was in a minority of one, however. Before we had even crossed the river to the north side of the city the forces of social control were hard at work. The lads insisted I would need to find new headgear before we arrived at the match venue, otherwise I would have to enter and leave on my own. Reluctantly, I assented.

It is a myth among GAA people countrywide that the Dubs do not like to travel to matches. Those that find themselves needing to leave home early in the morning in order to get to a game in the mid-afternoon often cast envious glances at the Dubs as they stroll down the North Circular Road, stopping off for a pint on the way before popping in to Croke Park for the afternoon's game. When, in later years, the new system of qualifiers would see the Dubs playing in far-flung counties like Monaghan, Laois and Tipperary, many would rub their hands in glee and advance theories as to how the park would, inevitably, be half empty because the Dubs would get lost once the road on either side of them became flanked with fields. In fact, the Dubs enjoy getting out and seeing the countryside, and Dublin have an enviable record on the road, having won some epic away games, notably the 1983 All-Ireland semi-final replay in Cork.

For many Dubs, the thought of a day in the country, a few pints with the lads, a match and a chance to scare the locals was all one could ask for. 'Hill 16 on Tour' was a different experience from Hill 16 itself, but not necessarily a lesser one.

In reality, many if not most of those who follow the Dubs are at most one generation removed from country life. Of the lads in the car with me that day, I was the only one to have had both my parents born in Dublin. I knew of one family in which the brothers that were old enough to remember their life in Kerry supported that county, while the younger brother was a fervent Dubs fan. This, in a sense, reflected the function which the Dublin team played in Dublin identity and had played since the '70s. Ciaran Walsh later described to me the scene he had witnessed as an eight year old, on the day Dublin won the 1974 All-Ireland final. His mother brought him to a field near his home where a huge bonfire had been lit and a crowd assembled to greet the victorious Dublin team. All around him were young lads his own age with their parents, many of whom hailed from Cork, Tipperary, Sligo, Donegal and throughout the country. 'There were a lot of country people,' he later remembered, 'a lot of country people who had moved into the area and all their kids were now Dubs. It was a chance to belong. To this day I still meet fellas who say "I'm 45 years living in Dublin, I'm a Corkman, but all my three sons are Dubs, and if the Dubs are playing anyone but Cork, then I'm a Dub too."'

In the US of the 1930s and 1940s, baseball was the way for many of the second-generation children of white immigrants to feel part of American culture. Players like Johnny Pesky (Paveskovich), Tommy Henrich and Phil Rizzuto, with parents from Croatia, Germany and Italy, all became stars for American kids to look up to. The baseball player who became one of the greatest ever American icons – Joe DiMaggio – was one of three baseball-playing sons of an immigrant Italian fisherman. In the early 1970s, Gaelic football came to perform a similar function for those who had migrated from rural Ireland to the ever-expanding Dublin. Walsh's own mother had come from Cork and he learned much of his craft playing football during his summers there. The father of Walsh's teammate Paul Curran had played football with Meath, Dessie Farrell's family came from Donegal while the great Brian Mullins was a nephew of Bill Casey who had played for Kerry in 1947, the year that the All-Ireland final was played in the Polo Grounds in New York. Wherever they came from and whatever their links, supporting the Dubs gave them all a chance to belong in Dublin and helped to give this new generation of city folk a collective identity.

We parked the car along by the banks of the river and walked up into the town, stretching the legs as we went. Although early in the day, Navan was starting to fill up with Dublin, Laois and some

Kildare jerseys (the Kildare underage team were playing Laois in the curtain-raiser). The ability of rival fans to mix with each other before, after and during Gaelic matches is something that is often confusing to those unfamiliar with the game. Whatever violence the two teams may inflict upon each other on the pitch, the rival fans sit alongside each other at the game and mingle on their way to and from it. This fact is all the more noteworthy when one considers the considerable level of alcohol some people imbibe on their way to matches and the lurid violence that often sweeps through the drunken crowds in Irish towns and cities most Saturday nights.

Paddy Russell, who would referee the 1995 football final, was once appointed to referee an exhibition match between Cork and Mayo held in Bradford City's football ground in England. He was amused when the police visited him before the game to inform him of a password which would be used to signal the abandonment of the game if crowd violence got out of hand. Later it was the police that were amazed as both sets of supporters wandered into the ground chatting happily with each other. That was simply the GAA way and that was the way it was in Navan that Sunday afternoon. The different groups of fans mingled easily, merrily swapping insults with each other as we turned into the town.

The main street in Navan looked like a cross between a carnival and a scene from *Dawn of the Dead*. All along the street were the brightly coloured carnival jesters. Most were decked out in the navy and sky-blue colours of the Dubs, many wearing replica jerseys. Among the Laois and Kildare fans it was largely the younger people who wore replica jerseys, but they were worn by Dubs of all ages and sizes. While, among soccer fans, it is often fashionable to have the most recent jersey, among the Dubs the older the jersey is, the better. An older jersey is a sign of your long-term commitment and suffering. Most of us had jerseys with the name of the Dublin sponsor 'Arnotts' (a Dublin department store) emblazoned across the front, but those who had a jersey from the days when Dublin was sponsored by 'Kaliber alcohol-free beer' were regarded as long-suffering indeed, while those whose jerseys pre-dated sponsorship were regarded as almost Christ-like. As we turned into the main street of Navan we were passed by one man in a jersey so old it must have pre-dated the replica jersey phenomenon itself. The jersey in question was stretched as tight as a drum across a vast gut and was partially hidden behind an extensive greying beard. We nodded in approval at the Dub – clearly the original of the species – and wondered if we too would look like that in 30 years' time.

Mixed in among the carnival, groups of men lurched about the place like zombies, displaying the characteristic gait of those who are suffering in the morning, having drunk too much the night before. The sun was beaming down on them without mercy for those whose eyes and head were not equipped for such bright light so early on the day after. Some had gathered in the shade of a nearby chip van – one of a number which dotted the street – and struggled to speak or be heard over the loud hum coming from the van's electric generator. They were the lucky ones. Most of the rest simply baked painfully in the sun.

Our group split up as some of us headed in search of lunch while the rest, nursing sore heads, headed in search of a cure for the previous night's hangover. Navan, it quickly transpired, was intent on doing little to give rise to any speculation that it might be an up-and-coming culinary Mecca. A decent sit-down meal appeared to be beyond the town, not least because the thought of thousands of Dubs descending on its streets had led the owners of whatever cafés existed to abandon their counters and leave the business to the pubs. There were a number of chip vans serving up a heady cocktail of chips, burgers and botulism, but we eventually opted instead to join the queue outside an overburdened fast-food joint and I settled for half eating a vegetarian kebab before leaving the remainder sitting on top of a public bin which was already spilling over with food waste. I drank a can of fizzy orange in order to try to wash the greasy taste from my mouth and we set off to join the rest of the lads in one of Navan's bars. On the way, I stopped to pick up a hat. All along the street, vendors competed with each other to attract our attention, aiming to sell a selection of novelty jester hats and Viking helmets as well as the more utilitarian baseball caps, all in the colours of the various county teams. I bought a straw cowboy-style hat with the blue and navy Dublin colours in plaited wool wrapped around it. The lads groaned that this was no better than the panama that had been left in the car but their opposition only convinced me that I had to buy it. Suitably attired, we joined the rest of our party in a local bar.

We found the lads in one of the quieter and darker pubs in Navan that day. It was at the far end of the town from the football ground and the lads were sitting near to the entrance. The only other group of football fans in the bar, a group of Dubs who had already had their fair share of drink, were at the far end of the room. While our lads were quietly sipping their pints and considering whether or not it was dark enough to risk taking off their sunglasses, the other Dubs were loudly projecting their views on the day's match at the backs of a couple of elderly Meath men who were sitting at the bar trying to read their Sunday papers.

'We'll hammer this lot today, and your lot the next day,' said one to the row of backs that faced him along the bar. They ignored him, and he tried again.

'Jaysus! I don't know why they even let teams like bleedin' Laois into the championship. Sure what chance do they have of winning it, huh? They should have, like, a second competition for shite teams.'

'They do,' said his mate, 'it's called "the hurling", and they're shite at that too.' This brought a cackle of laughter from the group, who chose to ignore Dublin's own less than stellar status in the hurling. No matter how bad Dublin were at the hurling, Meath were undoubtedly worse, so they continued to feel they were on safe ground. One of the old men evidently decided that he wasn't going to be left to read his paper in peace today. He drained the last of his pint, stood up while folding his newspaper slowly and began to walk to the door.

'Look,' said one of the Dubs, pointing at the retreating pensioner. 'That's your man, whatshisname? Your man from the telly. Colm O'Rourke.' Another cackle of laughter. Colm O'Rourke was Meath's corner-forward, a legendary player with exceptional accuracy, strength and controlled aggression. He was also a television pundit. He had terrorised Dublin's defence on many occasion but was now in his 19th championship season in Gaelic football and was one of the oldest players in the game. This jibe, at last, brought a response. The elderly Meath man stopped at the door and turned around.

'I hope ye win today lads,' he called back to his antagonisers. The loudest of them stood up and raised his pint glass to the old man in a belatedly respectful gesture of thanks.

'I hope ye win today, because I want to see Meath beat the stuffing out of you in the Leinster final,' the old man finished and, before anyone could come up with a reply, he had scampered out the door with surprising agility.

'They fucking might, you know,' one of the lads muttered dryly. While Dublin had faced down Louth, Meath had carved a swathe through the other side of the draw, beating Offaly by ten points and beating Longford 4–15 to 0–10. The previous week they had scored 3–14 to Wicklow's 0–9 in the other Leinster semi-final. Colm O'Rourke, who had started as a substitute in their first match, had scored three goals and six points already in the championship and was now waiting with his teammates to see who would win between Dublin and Laois. Laois were a tough enough team and Dublin would find it hard to beat them, but Meath were the bear pit.

We headed up to the ground in time to see the second half of the curtain-raising game. None of us had tickets but they were still on sale from a caravan outside the football ground. Arranging a queuing system was evidently beyond the capacities of the match organisers and so we joined the melee of bodies around the little caravan's window, holding money aloft before we joined the scrum, knowing there was no way to get your hands near to your pockets once you were in the middle of it. There was no point in trying to be polite and waiting your turn in this sort of scrum, so I drove myself forward through the crowd. Luckily I was tall enough to be able to see over the heads of many others in the crowd and, once I got close enough to the caravan, I fixed my gaze on the eyes of one of the sellers and waited until I had eye contact. I had learned while working behind a bar that many people at the front of the queue get careless or distracted and do not watch the seller carefully enough. Sure enough, within a minute or two I had purchased my ticket over the heads of some of those still in front of me. I pushed my way back out of the throng and we headed inside the park and took up our positions on the grassy terrace behind the goal.

As the enemy of my enemy is my friend, we decided to cheer for Kildare in the first match. Today was all about beating Laois after all, and we didn't care who beat them. We half hoped that if Laois took a good hammering in the first match it would be an omen for the main game. The teams were level at half-time, but Kildare played much better for most of the second half and were leading by four points in the last few minutes. By this stage, the crowd had swelled to almost 30,000 as the town's pubs emptied and people made their way into the ground. As the crowd grew, it became restless and anxious. One bunch of the travelling supporters began to chant, 'Bring on the Dubs!', ignoring the game that was going on in front of them. 'Come on. Get rid of this shite. Bring on the Dubs!' one guy shouted loud enough to be heard at the far side of the ground. We were shifting from foot to foot now, checking watches, as anxiety levels rose. 'How much left in this?' someone asked. 'Last minute,' came the reply.

Then a Laois player was fouled in the square and the referee signalled for a penalty. Laois midfielder Ian Fitzgerald drove it home, and suddenly Laois were only a point down. The ball was kicked out again and the same player went down a second time, this time winning a free. This time Fitzgerald drilled it over the bar and the match was level. The referee blew his whistle: game over. Shit. Laois had seemed well beaten and had scored a goal and a point in one minute to level the match. Now we hoped that it would not be an omen for the big game.

Dublin had good cause to fear Laois. They had three or four good forwards, men such as Hughie Emerson, Damien Delaney and Leo Turley. They were solid around midfield. If they had a weakness it was in their defence which, perhaps, was not the biggest bunch of players on the pitch. Unfortunately, Dublin's Achilles heel had traditionally been in attack, so while their defence might not be great, it could be enough to unsettle our forwards. Laois had in the past a name for being ill-disciplined, for giving up on the game and concentrating on the fight before the game was over. Recent years had seen that element removed from their game, however, and it seemed likely that this time they would play football for the whole game. They had come through two close games against Carlow and would have learned a lot about themselves in the process. Dublin, on the other hand, had faced only a fairly ragged Louth and had even let them back into the game before finally killing them off. 'I don't like this. I don't like this one little bit,' one of the lads muttered to himself, shifting anxiously from foot to foot. No one said anything in reply.

Ciaran Walsh had not needed to wait that long for his spot in the team. In the days before the game, Dermot Deasy's hamstring injury flared up, meaning that he would not be fit to play on Sunday. Walsh, who had some experience of playing in the centre of the last line of defence, was told that he would take Deasy's place and would mark Damien Delaney. Keith Barr's position had not been filled when the team was announced on the Tuesday before the game and the match programme listed 'A.N. Other' in his position. He came through a late fitness test, however, and when his participation in the game was announced, it was greeted with a large and relieved roar of approval from the Dublin fans.

The fans were nervous, too, though. Young Keith Galvin was set to defend against Leo Turley, a man twice his size. Galvin was evidently full of confidence, but he was still a teenager in only his second big match. There was a fear among the crowd that Turley might simply crush him like a bug. At midfield, we felt that Brian Stynes and Paul Bealin would be more than capable of matching their direct opponents. Stynes was the brother of Jim Stynes, the Gaelic footballer who had gone to Australia and become one of Australian Rules football's all-time most decorated players. Brian too had spent time in Australia before returning to play for Dublin. He looked a bigger, stronger player this year and had a phenomenal capacity to cover every inch of the pitch. He was also a ball winner, someone who you could count on to raise his game when the going was tough. Bealin was a decent foil for Stynes, a hard-working if sometimes uninspiring player. Midfield had long been a concern for Dublin, and a number of players had been tried there. It remained to be seen if Bealin was the partner that Stynes needed.

In attack, Dessie Farrell had been moved away from goal into the half-forward line, the position in which he had proved his effectiveness in the previous match. Paul Clarke also started at wing-forward and Sean Cahill, who had been substituted after only 20 minutes against Louth, got another chance in the half-forward line. Mick Galvin had been moved into full-forward alongside Charlie Redmond and young Jason Sherlock, who was getting his first championship start.

It was hard to know what to make of the forwards. On the

evidence of the last day it was hard to see Cahill being the answer to Dublin's prayers, and the fact that they were persisting with him at all suggested to the fans that the Dubs resources up front must be quite thin. Paul Clarke had played well the last day but it remained to be seen if he would be consistent. Clarke was known to the fans as 'Clarkey' but to his teammates he was sometimes known as 'Merlin'. This was because, in training, when faced with a decision between the simple move and one that would require magical powers to execute, Merlin always tried to be the magician. There were moments on the pitch when he was an exquisite footballer but there were also others when his touch and composure seemed to desert him. Which Paul Clarke would turn up still had to be confirmed. There was no concern about Dessie Farrell or Mick Galvin, and Charlie Redmond seemed to have bounced back over the winter from the torment of the previous September, even if the decision not to have him take the penalty against Louth suggested a lingering mental frailty.

That left Sherlock. He had done well in the previous match when coming off the bench, but he looked so small and light out there that it seemed only a matter of time before some mullocking corner-back simply broke him clean in two and posted the bits back to Dublin GAA headquarters in separate parcels. There was no doubt he made space for himself well, that he could win the ball, had good vision and could distribute the ball as well. On the evidence of his first game, however, it was less clear that he could actually solo the ball or that he could shoot a point. Yet, before he had even played in a senior championship game the media had been talking him up and it seemed no article had been written about Dublin football the previous week that had not been adorned with his picture. Having shown only flashes of brilliance, he was being made into the long-awaited saviour of Dublin football, and the hopes of tens of thousands were now saddled to his narrow young shoulders. It was hard to imagine someone not yet 20 carrying that weight.

The match was to be refereed by Brian White from Wexford. 'Aw, fuck!' someone exclaimed. 'Not Brian White! That's at least a three-point advantage to Laois already.'

'That bastard,' someone else spat. In fact it hardly mattered who was refereeing the game, because it would always be assumed that the referee was out to get Dublin. The referee always came from a 'neutral' county, but, since it was taken for granted that all the culchies were united by their desire to see Dublin lose, this meant that all referees were against Dublin. In the cold light of day, most people would find this belief hard to justify on the basis of any evidence, but this wasn't the cold light of day, it was the blazing heat of a championship Sunday, and all conspiracy theories suddenly sounded reasonable. 'Where's your hairdryer, you prick?' someone shouted at the ref and got a laugh from the crowd. Brian White had black, wavy hair that always looked immaculately groomed. This, in itself, became one more ground for suspicion.

Laois started quickly and went a point up inside the first minute. Damien Delaney got free of Ciaran Walsh with almost the first attack of the game and suddenly found himself in acres of space in front of the Dublin goal. Luckily for Dublin he blasted his shot and missed. A moment later he had left Walsh for dead again and scored a point. Laois were playing with the wind, and things were tight in the middle of the pitch with both teams crowding out the space. Laois got a free which Delaney scored and they were two up. A Dublin player took a knock which should have been a free-kick but the referee didn't see it. The abuse started. 'What match are you looking at, you wanker!' I heard myself shout, the pitch of my voice rising all the time. Almost immediately he gave a free against Dublin. 'You saw that all right, didn't you, you fucking hairdresser,' one of the lads shouted, spittle flying from his mouth and spraying those standing in front of us. 'Fucking . . .' I said, getting no further before seething anger strangled the rest of the words. My fists were clenched and I made myself take a deep breath. 'Come on, Dubs, for fuck sake!' I roared.

Dublin started to come back into it: Paul Clarke scored a point, then Charlie got a free-kick. Walsh started to get the better of Delaney while Paddy Moran and Keith Galvin had swapped corners, and Moran was holding Leo Turley well. The game swung back and forth like a see-saw. Laois were generally on top, their half-forwards and midfield winning more possession. Although they were missing a few frees, they managed to go two points up again. But Dublin dragged themselves back into it. Sherlock burst through the centre, taking a neat pass from Charlie Redmond and panic ensued in the Laois defence just in front of us. Sherlock opted for placement over power and neatly side-footed the ball past the Laois keeper. For a delicious moment it looked to have gone in the net, but it cannoned back off the post and into play. Nonetheless, a buzz started to spread among the Dublin players and the fans gathered behind the goal. Sherlock had set a fire among sections of the Dublin crowd and the singing started again: 'Come on you boys in blue . . .' Dublin drew level, then went a point up before Laois equalised late in the half. Laois had played the better football and really should have been in front but Dublin had stayed with them and would be playing with the wind in the second half.

Dublin started the second half better than Laois. The Dublin half-back line of Paul Curran, Keith Barr and Mick Deegan were doing better at closing down the Laois half-forward line and shutting off their team's supply of possession. But they were getting themselves booked by the referee in the process and still Laois had not been silenced. Hughie Emerson caught a clean ball just in front of the Dublin goal but once more it was blasted wide. Laois had now blasted and missed from two good positions in front of goal. Against more composed opposition Dublin might well have been two goals down. Ten thousand throats issued a collective sigh of relief from behind the goal. Down in front of us on the grassy terrace a bunch of fans started to taunt Emerson: 'He shot, he missed, he must be fucking pissed, glory-oh, glory-oh,' they sang. Most of us, however, concentrated on the Dubs: 'Come on, Dubs, let's put this shower away! For fuck sake! Show what you are made of!' Advice was being liberally offered now. Dublin broke down a Laois attack and started to hand-pass the ball out of defence but Laois kept them under pressure.

'What are you doing? Stop fannying around with it. Just kick the fucking thing. It's called *foot*ball, you fucking muppet,' someone near us shouted.

Laois were strangling the centre of the field, crowding it out with bodies and fighting furiously to gain possession of each loose ball. But they had made chances and failed to take them. Dublin, who should have been dead and buried by now, started to gain a foothold in the centre of the pitch. Paul Clarke scored for Dublin, then once more, and Dublin were two points clear. Dessie Farrell had by now abandoned the overcrowded centre half-forward position and moved onto the wing, where he was picking up greater possession. Two more points in quick succession and Dublin were four points up. Laois were not finished yet, however. Delaney scored two more frees and once more Dublin were only two points clear. Some of the abuse hurled by the Dublin fans at their players was by now personal and some of it was downright nasty. 'That fucking Jap hasn't done anything,' someone in the crowd away to our right said loudly, as Sherlock failed to reach a ball. A few minutes later Sherlock went for another ball and got hit with a heavy but fair shoulder by a Laois player. 'That was like Hiroshima all over again,' laughed the racist to our right, before adding, 'Come on, take him off. They don't play football the same way in fucking Tokyo.' The lads and I were looking at each other, uneasy, not knowing how to respond to such abuse, when a voice from behind the racist growled at him, 'Shut your fucking mouth. He's a Dub. He's from Dublin.' There was a moment of tension on the terrace as people waited to hear the nature of the response, but the racist just mumbled quietly to himself and the shouting stopped. I breathed a sigh of relief, both because the abuse had been challenged and because there was not going to be a fight. Both teams scored again and, as the game entered its last 15 minutes, Dublin were only two points clear. Neither Sherlock nor Cahill had scored and the match hung in the balance. In the crowd, we bit our fingernails and barked at our team. The singing had almost died out. They say that in the trenches there are no atheists. These were the trenches and we were praying.

Then came the moment that would be played on television over and again all that summer, the first in the series of cameos that would turn young Jason Sherlock into Jayo, folk hero and the first GAA superstar. Jim Gavin had replaced Mick Galvin in the Dublin attack and, with what seemed to be his first touch of the ball, he lofted a pass into the space in front of Sherlock. Jason, who had probably been lucky not to have been replaced himself, got to the ball at the same time as a Laois player got to him. The Laois player's foot landed on Sherlock's boot, pinning it to the turf. Perhaps he thought that without the use of his foot Sherlock could go nowhere but, in the twinkling of an eye, Sherlock twisted free of boot and marker and set off like blue lightning towards goal, his lost boot bouncing along behind him and the Laois defence trailing in his wake. Before anyone could react, he let fly from an acute angle with his stockinged foot and crashed the ball past the goalkeeper and, from the far end of the pitch, we could see the net bulge and dance. The Dublin fans gathered on the grassy slope erupted and danced and hugged each other. Sherlock fell to his knees facing them, arms aloft, inviting acclaim in the sort of gesture that is common for soccer players when they score but which is largely unheard of in Gaelic football. Old man Charlie Redmond gruffly picked him up and placed him back on his feet before slapping him on the back while, at the far end of the park, ten thousand voices began to ring out, 'Jay-o! Jay-o!' Almost immediately Mick Deegan burst forward from the half-back line and tacked on another point as Dublin pressed home their advantage. As in the earlier game, a goal and a point in the space of a minute changed the complexion of the match completely and, with a bound, Dublin were free. Six points clear with ten minutes to go and we had found our voice. There was no way Dublin will let this lead slip. This game was over.

Mick Lawlor of Laois responded with a point, but Sherlock was not finished yet. With three minutes to go, he spotted Dublin substitute Vinnie Murphy on a charge through the centre and picked him out with a perceptive pass. For a second, it looked as if another goal was on but Murphy blasted the ball over the bar. Charlie wrapped up proceedings with another free, bringing his total to seven scores (all points, six from frees), but the only person anyone wanted to talk about was Jayo. Charlie's scores were the difference between the two teams but Jayo's goal had changed the game at a crucial time for Dublin. More than that, he had brought back the swagger to the team, what Tom Humphries in the following day's *Irish Times* would refer to as 'the sort of flair which Dublin have pined for since the end of the seventies'.

The Laois team of 1995 were good enough to beat all except the top two or three sides in the country and could probably have beaten all six of the teams that were to contest the provincial finals in the other three provinces that year, but the geographical accident that trapped them in Leinster behind Dublin and Meath ensured that no one would afterwards remember 1995 as the year of an excellent Laois side. Dublin would now move on to face Meath in the Leinster final and Humphries noted that a 'snarling dog-fight of a Leinster final awaits us'.

As the team retreated from Navan and turned their thoughts to the next game against Meath, there was some time for a sense of quiet satisfaction. They had come through a very tough game and had twice now shown a clinical ability to finish the opposition off when the opportunity presented itself. In Jason Sherlock they had also a new and unpredictable quality that opposing teams had not heretofore encountered. With Dessie on the half-forward line and Jim Gavin coming into the team, the attack seemed to have a better balance. Overall, it looked like a team capable of mounting a championship challenge was taking shape.

The picture was not so positive for all the players, however. Sean Cahill had started both the Louth game and the Laois game, but had not made the desired impact. A big, fit and quick player, who matched this physical ability with strong football skills, he perhaps seemed better suited to midfield but had tended to be picked in the forwards. Although he had been given almost the whole game on this occasion and had failed to register a score, some of his shots had drifted very narrowly wide. Looking back on it, more than a decade later, Dessie Farrell was struck by how unlucky he had been: 'He was one of those players: it just didn't happen for him, but he was very close. There have probably been a couple of players in a similar position over the years, and that year it was him. He was unfortunate, because he was very close and probably could have come off the pitch that day scoring three points as easily as scoring nothing. But for him, that was it. He was unheard of then after that.'

Four

Me and the Devil Blues

IN EARLY JUNE 1991, I travelled from Ireland to the US on a student summer work visa. I was to spend the summer working as an intern in the Federal Department of Health and Human Services, two blocks from the Capitol building in Washington DC. This, of course, was back in the days before 'working as an intern in DC' took on Lewinsky connotations. I was 19 years old, had never been on an aeroplane and had never lived away from home for longer than three weeks before.

I was met at Washington's National Airport by some relations of a colleague of my father's. Since I knew no one in DC – indeed, since I knew no one within a thousand kilometres of DC – they had agreed to meet me and help me get on my feet when I arrived. I approached this meeting with some trepidation since I didn't quite know what 'get on my feet' would mean. It was possible that all they were going to do was sit me down over a cup of coffee and set me straight on a few things before waving goodbye and setting me loose on the mean streets of the city which was at the time the murder capital of the Western world.

As it turned out, they were a family of unusual kindness and decency. They welcomed me into their home in Silver Spring, a Maryland suburb of DC, and for the best part of two months treated me as one of the family. They introduced me to other Irish people in DC and I began to feel less isolated, less lost and alone. Contact with other Irish people and with Irish-Americans ensured that I had some common reference points, something to talk about. They could explain to me how things worked there because, being aware of both the US and Ireland, they understood the differences that would give rise to confusion. I knew I was staying in the US for only four months but the sense of isolation was still oppressive. Some days I would walk back to their house from the bus stop and imagine myself in DC and my home in Ireland as seen from space, just two specks on different continents, thousands of kilometres apart. The feeling of being alone would almost overpower me. Meeting Irish people settled in the US and making lives for themselves gave me a sense of confidence that I could get on OK.

One early summer evening in the house in Maryland someone told me that the local GAA team were training nearby and asked if I wanted to come along. I could scarcely believe my ears. We walked down the hill through the suburbs of Silver Spring and then across the baseball diamond, where the sight of lads soloing and hand-passing the ball and kicking points seemed like a mirage in front of me. But there it was. As wives and children sat and talked and played on the slope overlooking the field, there was a bunch of Irish and Irish-American lads acting out one of Ireland's rituals, more than 5,000 kilometres from home.

If I was to look for the precise moment when my love affair with Gaelic football began, that was it. I went to the US as someone who had next to no interest in Gaelic games. I had played a bit in school but had done so with some reluctance. Like most gangly teenagers around the onset of puberty, I lacked some grace and coordination. More than that, my self-doubt in social situations meant I lived in constant fear that my next touch of the ball would result in some catastrophe or other which my teammates would never forgive. I was actually a half-decent goalkeeper, and, being tall, wiry and pretty fearless on the pitch, I had once been spotted by a coach of some renown who told me I would make a good midfielder if I learned to judge the flight of the ball better, but my lack of self-confidence and my fear of making a terrible gaffe made matches a torment. When school no longer required it, I was more than happy to disengage fully from sport. By 1991 that had changed somewhat, as I had spent the previous three years cheering on the national soccer team, but my interest had not stretched to Gaelic football. Thousands of miles from my nearest friend, however, Gaelic football seemed like home.

The lads I played with in the States were a mixed bag. There was at least one who had played inter-county championship football in his heyday (now a few years past) and a couple of other younger lads who maybe could have played championship football if they hadn't ended up emigrating. There was also a bunch who, like me, had rudimentary skills, knew the rules and had picked up basic tactics as much by osmosis as by design. There were also a bunch of Irish-Americans who had grown up playing baseball but who were searching for a root and who found it while trying to solo a ball across a rock-hard, bone-dry Maryland pitch. Training was a loosely organised affair at that time of the year and sometimes there weren't enough people to play a practice match. On those days, we mixed in with the Mexicans who were on the pitch next to us and played soccer with them. On other days, enough people turned up and we trained for football: passing, moving, tackling and shooting in the hazy sunshine of a summer's evening.

I had flown out to the US on 4 June 1991. Two days previously, Dublin and Meath had drawn a first-round championship match in Croke Park. The match barely registered with me as I packed and planned to be off. The match was not on television, so, unless you were there or unless you were interested in the first place, it did not reach out and grab your attention. No one could have known at the time that this was just the beginning of what the

GAA historian Jack Mahon would later call Gaelic football's greatest saga.

To say that Dublin and Meath were each other's greatest rivals does not come close to articulating what goes on between these two neighbours. There were other great rivalries in Gaelic football, such as Mayo and Galway in the west, or Kerry and Cork in the south, or, indeed, any number of pairings in Ulster. Hurling also had its own special rivalry in Cork and Tipperary. In all these cases there was the rivalry of a derby game between near neighbours, both of whom had a proud history to defend. With Dublin and Meath there was all this, but there was more. Both teams were among the best in the country, with a wealth of skilful players. On the Meath team, players such as Mick Lyons, Liam Hayes, Brian Stafford and Colm O'Rourke were regarded as among the best of their generation. O'Rourke in particular was a legend. For most top players, their championship career lasts, at most, a few years. For amateur sportsmen, the demands of their day job make training difficult over a long period. The tough, physical nature of Gaelic football also ensures that injuries and wear and tear shorten a player's career. The normal ups and downs of form mean that few players sustain performances that would allow them to be consistently picked for the county over an extended period of time. Yet O'Rourke's career by 1991 spanned 16 years since his first championship start in 1976. He was gifted with many of the physical attributes that make a good footballer. He was physically strong, a good ball winner with good balance and superb shooting accuracy. He also had excellent football intelligence, was someone who could read a game, identify a team's strengths and weaknesses and plot their downfall while the thunder and lightning of a championship encounter was happening all around.

But Dublin and Meath were more than just skilful opponents. When Michael Cusack set out to found Gaelic games, it was in part because he felt that the other sporting codes lacked the physically bruising nature of the games he had seen in the Clare of his youth. Dublin and Meath played as if they were out to turn his dream into a nightmare. Meath in particular seemed possessed by an iron will and a ruthless determination to win. Since the mid-1980s, O'Rourke and Meath had been like the Terminator: they could not be bargained with, they could not be reasoned with and they absolutely, positively would not stop until their objective had been achieved or they had been crushed. They were at their most dangerous when they were behind with a few minutes to go on the clock. Another team would get disheartened and their heads would drop, but not Meath. They were not a team that lost a game, they were only ever beaten.

Meath were managed by Sean Boylan, a diminutive, genial and soft-spoken man who never failed to charm the public or the television cameras when they crossed his path. Yet this affable character clearly also had a darker side because the teams he built were possessed by a determination that, on occasion, verged on the psychopathological. Claustrophobic and feral encounters with Dublin in the 1980s had forged them into a honed and flint-like unit which became bonded together with the glue of paranoia. When they believed that everybody hated them, it made them stronger. Indeed, their brand of football was generally far from pretty and the term most often used in the media to describe them was probably 'grim killer instinct'. But, if it was not attractive, it was effective and had won them two All-Ireland titles in the previous few years. Although individually the players were often highly regarded as decent and engaging souls, collectively they became a bunch of people you would not like to meet at night in a dark alley. Meeting them in a dark alley at night, however, was infinitely preferable to meeting them on a warm summer's Sunday on a Gaelic football pitch.

Dublin brought this quality out in them more than any other opponent. On the pitch, the contest was bone-jarring and teeth-rattling. Two bunches of hard men stood toe to toe and would give and ask no quarter. They hit each other hard, on and off the ball, and sought to win possession and scores by physically dominating the opposition and by psychologically intimidating them. Players would measure their contribution to the game by the amount of pain they were suffering and they knew that if they weren't hurting it was because they weren't in the game. O'Rourke later wrote, 'To get the sort of respect from backs that allows you to play means that you have to "bust" a few of them in high-profile games, and the word quickly spreads around that any back grabbing your jersey runs the risk of having a few teeth dislodged.' This was the attitude which both the Meath and Dublin teams brought to their encounters. In the old western movie *A Man Called Horse,* Richard Harris joins a Native American tribe in which a young male could only become a man after he had gone through a ritual which involved tethering his nipples to a post by piercing them with an animal tooth and then dragging his body backwards until he ripped himself free. For those who played in games between Dublin and Meath, they too were a kind of scarring ritual, a rite of passage. Men faced an intensity of physical pain and did not wilt, and in doing so found out what they were capable of.

The third element that made Dublin against Meath special was Croke Park. The imposing old stadium was Gaelic football's greatest stage and playing there was one of the game's highest honours. Like a priest being invited to say Mass in the Sistine Chapel, everybody knew that this was their moment to shine or to fade away. Croke Park at the time held 64,000 people, almost 2 per cent of the population of the country, and the crowd turned the pitch into a goldfish bowl as they roared abuse and approval, or sometimes just roared. Sometimes the crowd was so loud that players could not hear the referee's whistle or their teammate's shouts. Surrounded by a dizzying array of colour and noise as Dublin's blue and navy contested the skyline with Meath's green and gold, players knew at every moment that the attention, the

The Dublin team before the 1995 All-Ireland final. Charlie Redmond (front row, far right) was still wearing his tracksuit when the photo was taken, as it was still not clear whether he was fit to play.

Paul Clarke leaps and punches the goal that wins Dublin the 1995 Leinster final. The game – and the goal – will live long in the memory of supporters of both Dublin and Meath.

Keith Barr strikes the penalty in the last match of the 1991 Dublin and Meath saga and blasts it narrowly wide. The penalty miss was central to Dublin losing the greatest epic in the history of Gaelic games.

Dublin play Meath in 1995 on the day the New Stand is opened.
The New Stand dwarfed the old and signalled the re-birth of Croke Park.

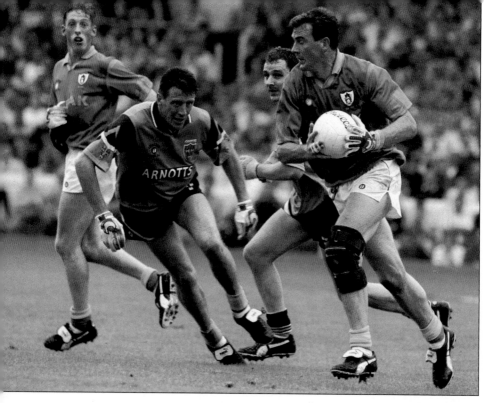

The legendary Colm O'Rourke takes on Dublin's Jack Sheedy in the 1994 championship, while Ciaran Walsh and Meath's Trevor Giles look on. O'Rourke's age and his perpetually strapped knee belied his ability and determination.

Dublin captain and goalkeeper John O'Leary drove the team forward.

Dublin's Brian Stynes and Cork's Liam Honohan contest the ball in the 1995 All-Ireland semi-final, while Dublin's Paul Clarke (number 11) and Dessie Farrell prepare to mop up any breaking ball.

Jason Sherlock crashes the ball past Kevin O'Dwyer in the Cork net for the decisive score in the 1995 All-Ireland semi-final. Behind Sherlock, the crowd leans forward in anticipation and despair.

Peter Canavan, who achieved a point-scoring record in the 1995 All-Ireland final and whose grace, ability and determination set him apart as one of the finest players ever to have played Gaelic football.

Referee Paddy Russell points to the line a second time to indicate to Charlie Redmond that he had been sent off after all in the All-Ireland final, 1995.

Ciaran Walsh holds his arms aloft to celebrate the All-Ireland victory of 1995,
while behind him the crowd take the field.

When Hill 16 is in full voice, the noise rolls like thunder around the ground. Even now, after
the redesign of the stadium, the Hill remains an elemental force.

hopes and the dreams of every person in the ground and millions more throughout the country and worldwide were focused on their next shot, their next tackle, their next decision. In such a cauldron it sometimes happened that strong men felt weak while fast men discovered that their legs weighed a ton and that their chest tightened as they fought for air. Some cracked under the pressure and did something rash or violent that hurt their own team. For others, the pressure brought adrenalin which enabled them to run faster, hit harder, think and play smarter and make it through the pain.

Dublin and Meath's rivalry was based on a familiarity like no other. They had played each other in every Leinster final between 1986 and 1990. There was little between the teams on any of those occasions, although Dublin had won only once, in 1989. Although the provincial system at the time meant that Dublin and Meath would never play each other in an All-Ireland final, their games often had a greater intensity than the All-Ireland. O'Rourke later wrote that games against Dublin were the yardstick by which any Meath footballer would judge himself.

Draws are far less common in Gaelic football than in soccer. Like in rugby or basketball, the greater frequency of the scores in Gaelic football as compared with soccer means that it is not common for two teams to be deadlocked at the end of 70 minutes. As it happened, the draw between Dublin and Meath on 2 June 1991 was in itself a kind of freak occurrence. Dublin had been leading by five points after a tempestuous first half but had seen their lead whittled away as Meath's Liam Hayes came to life in the second half and dominated the centre of the field, winning possession time and again and creating scoring opportunities for his forwards. Nonetheless, Dublin were leading by a single point going into the last minute and looked to be heading for a famous victory when they lost possession out on their right touchline. P.J. Gillic for Meath pumped the ball in towards the Dublin goal and John O'Leary came out to challenge an inrushing Meath player. Both missed the ball and for a split second it looked as if it might bounce into the unguarded net, but it cleared the bar for a point. The game ended 1–12 to 1–12 and the two teams were required to meet again the following week. So the saga began.

It was at football training, ten days later that someone said to me, 'By the way, did you hear the news?'

'No,' I replied.

'They drew again. Can you believe it?'

'What?' I asked, a little confused.

'Dublin and Meath. They drew again: 0–10 each after normal time, 1–11 each after extra time.'

'How can you still be drawing in Gaelic football after two matches and extra time?'

'Dunno. I think they'll need a crowbar to separate them.'

Two weeks later, Dublin against Meath was all anyone was talking about at football training. Tapes of the radio coverage of the games were being passed around, and so even those of us on the far side of the world got to catch up within a few days.

'Dublin had their chance in the first game,' someone suggested, 'and Meath won't let them get another.'

'No. This Meath team are too old, too long in the tooth to be able to last the pace of three games like that,' someone else said.

'Jesus, those fellas are killing each other,' said a third.

'Maybe it's not age, it's just experience,' said an old head.

'I tell you what,' someone else ventured. 'I think Dublin will need to drive a stake through Meath's heart before you'll be sure they're beaten. And they'll need a crucifix and garlic just to make sure.'

Back at home, Ireland was going Gaelic football mad. A year previously, the nation had scarcely given the GAA a thought as the exploits of the national soccer team in Italia '90 had been the focus of attention. Now, Dublin and Meath had rescued the GAA just when it seemed to be losing its place in the nation's sporting consciousness to soccer, and the country went mad for Gaelic football as it had not done in over a decade. John O'Leary later wrote, 'People who five weeks previously knew nothing about Gaelic football were now discussing the relative merits of the respective half-backs. Dublin and Meath had opened a window to Gaelic football, and everybody wanted to peer inside.' Writing in the *Evening Press* that week, Con Houlihan was more concise: 'All Gaeldom looks on agog,' he wrote. Unbelievably, the third match was also drawn at the end of normal time and again after extra time. And so, after four and a half hours of football, it was back once more to Croke Park for the next replay on a Saturday in early July, over a month after the contest had first begun.

Sitting on the slope above the pitch in Maryland after training, we talked about the upcoming game as the sun set behind the trees. Some said that this match was the real All-Ireland final, that these two teams were better than anything else in the country. Some said it was bigger than the All-Ireland, that Dublin against Meath had taken on greater significance than the prize for which they were contesting. The All-Ireland is won every year after all, but 116 years of Gaelic games had never before produced anything to rival the Dublin and Meath saga of 1991. In years to come, it was said, many people will be unable to remember who won the All-Ireland in 1990 or 1992, but no one will forget this. The same conversation was happening, against the backdrop of different scenery, throughout Ireland and among Irish people in pubs in the UK, along Bondi beach in Australia and worldwide. People who had never imagined going to Croke Park made plans to watch the game. Over 20,000 replica Dublin jerseys were sold in the week before the game. For the first time ever, a first-round championship match was to be shown live on television in order that the whole country could watch in rapt fascination. The radio coverage of the game was to be re-broadcast on a local radio station in Washington DC. Saturday dawned bright and sunny. The crowds turned out and packed Croke Park, turning it into a cauldron of noise and colour. Jack Mahon later wrote in his *History of Gaelic Football*, 'It was the perfect day.'

And, at 5.05 that Saturday evening, it seemed to be the perfect day for Dublin. By then, the game was well into its second half and Dublin were six points clear, leading by 0–12 to 0–6. Meath were looking flat and it seemed as if the long struggle had finally told on their ageing bodies. Of course, Meath had come back from a five-point deficit previously in the series but at six points clear it looked that even if Dublin had not yet driven a stake through the beast's heart, they at least had the point of the stake in position and the mallet at the ready. The match had begun among what Colm O'Rourke later described as 'the greatest atmosphere of any I have ever played in . . . Just as the match was about to begin there was the greatest build-up of noise and expectation I have ever experienced in that Stadium of Light.' The match had exploded at breakneck speed and Meath had started well, knocking over a couple of points. Dublin had then come back into the game. O'Rourke went for a ball and was met by two Dublin players – Keith Barr and Eamon Heery – who hit him so hard that he had headaches for months afterwards. O'Rourke was dazed and Meath were in trouble. Dublin went in at half-time leading 0–7 to 0–5. They played much the better football in the early stages of the second half and, with 20 minutes to go, led by six.

Meath pulled back a point, and then a goal, but Dublin were still two points clear, and the team that had been forged in the flames of the previous five hours of football were not going to cave in now. Dublin kicked two more points before Meath hit back with one more. Going into the last few minutes, Dublin were three points clear at 0–14 to 1–8 (11 points). Then a Dublin player was dragged down in the box. It was a penalty.

Keith Barr had been the person nominated as the penalty taker in advance, and he stepped up to take it. In the days and weeks that followed, with the benefit of hindsight, Dublin fans would argue that Keith should have simply knocked the ball over the bar for a point, but the stake was still in position and Meath had yet to be slain. Others argued that Mick Lyons of Meath had distracted Keith by running alongside him as he ran up to take the shot, and that the referee should therefore have ordered the penalty to be retaken. Keith lashed his shot low and hard, with the intention of killing the tie off once and for all. The shot was close, so close in fact that the television commentator initially called it as a goal, but in fact it was centimetres wide. Dublin were not deflated by the miss and quickly scored another point – the insurance point that meant Meath needed two scores to draw level. Once more Meath came back, scoring a free, but going into the last two minutes Dublin were still a goal up.

When it was all over, and the Dublin players sat drained and tearful in their dressing-room, they would have to face the fact that the final, vital wounds were self-inflicted. Vinnie Murphy had the ball for Dublin in front of the Meath goal. Punching the ball over the bar for the insurance point would have been easy, but instead he sought to pass the ball to another Dublin player. It was intercepted by Meath's Martin O'Connell, who began the move up the pitch. Meath passed the ball around slowly at first before it came to O'Rourke. Perhaps realising that Dublin's defenders were slow in getting back into position, the Dublin corner-back, Mick Kennedy, slowed down play by clattering into and flattening O'Rourke. O'Rourke took the resultant free but the ball was played loosely and almost went over the sideline before David Beggy rescued it. Meanwhile one of the Meath defenders, Kevin Foley, had spotted the stewards starting to surround the pitch and knew that it was only a matter of seconds before the referee blew the final whistle. He bounded forward to join the attack and picked up the pass from Beggy. Dublin had men back now and, although they were not yet properly organised, there still seemed to be no real danger. Foley transferred the ball onto P.J. Gillic before starting to advance on the left-hand side, while Gillic – the man whose bounced point had started all the drama five weeks previously – moved the ball on to Tommy Dowd. Dowd was a bullish attacker and took the ball at speed. Suddenly, the Dublin defence sensed danger. Dowd interchanged passes with O'Rourke, taking defenders out of the game and, in a flash, was through on goal. Foley, who had started on the right-hand side of defence, now appeared alongside Dowd on the left-hand side of the attack and, as John O'Leary came out to narrow the angle for the shot, Dowd flicked a pass to Foley. O'Leary lunged at Foley but slipped at the vital moment and the ball flashed under him and into the net. O'Leary later said, 'I am convinced that if I hadn't slipped I would have got down on Foley's boot quite comfortably. Still, I was certain that I would be able to smother Foley's shot. I got down well but somehow – and I still don't know to this day how he managed it – Foley squeezed the ball underneath me and into the net.' The Meath fans in the stadium erupted in a frenzy while the Dublin fans were shell-shocked. Dublin could barely make sense of the horror that was unfolding in front of them, as seconds later Meath were tearing back up the wing before transferring the ball into a central attacking position. The Dublin defenders had now fallen into a shambles and Meath's David Beggy received the ball in acres of space and kicked them into a one-point lead. The beast had broken free. It could not be killed. Jack Sheedy had a last-minute chance to level it for Dublin but his long-range free-kick drifted wide, the referee blew the whistle and, finally, it was all over.

The Watergate burglar and right-wing American radio talk show host G. Gordon Liddy once wrote about how he had, over a period of time, built up his willpower by burning his own hand: 'I had begun by using lighted cigarettes, then matches and candles, progressively increasing the time I exposed my body to pain as I built up my will, much as one might build muscles by lifting increasingly heavy weights. By 1967 the exposure had become long enough to start leaving small permanent scars. Still I persisted, always using my left hand and forearm so as never to incapacitate my right – my gun-hand.' Like Liddy, Meath sought to play the game, not necessarily with superior skill, but with superior will. O'Rourke would later say that no team would ever have been allowed to score a goal against Meath like the one they had scored against Dublin. They would have stopped it with unflinching iron resolve, just as they had three times come back from the dead against Dublin through sheer determination. This question of will would haunt Dublin in the next few years. In 1992 they lost an All-Ireland final through lack of concentration. In 1993 they lost the semi-final by a single point, having led comfortably at half-time. In 1994, they had sufficient chances after the penalty miss to win the game but failed to take them. By the middle of the decade they had been the country's most consistent team and had nothing to show for it but a reputation for being the country's most celebrated losers. Everyone knew that the players had the skill. The question was whether they had the will.

G. Gordon Liddy later required surgery on his hand, after he held it over a candle so long that he cooked a finger joint and almost destroyed a tendon. For Meath, too, their triumph of will in 1991 came at a cost. In most years, a county might expect to be in an All-Ireland final after four games (indeed, in 1997 Kerry won the All-Ireland title having played only four games, none of them as gruelling as any of the Dublin and Meath matches in 1991). Meath had played in four matches – two with extra time added – and were still only through to the second round of the Leinster provincial championship. They stumbled through the rest of the championship, having enough class to beat almost all comers but without any real reserves of strength. While a younger team might have grown in strength from playing matches so regularly, Meath already had a lot of miles on the clock. In the All-Ireland final, they played Down, and lost by two points. Meath and Dublin had, like Sherlock Holmes and his nemesis Dr Moriarty, locked each other in a terrible grip and plunged through a cascading torrent that would ultimately prove fatal for both. Meath walked away from Croke Park in July as victors, but they were already mortally wounded. It just took them longer to die.

The saga of 1991 left a lasting impression on all those involved. In describing the last match of the four, O'Rouke later wrote that the goal brings him close to tears when he sees it replayed, and makes him want to jump for joy. The Dublin captain, Tommy Carr, described the loss as being like 'a death in the family' and no one begrudged him his exaggeration. But, while Charlie Redmond would remain haunted by his penalty miss in 1994, Keith Barr carries no such burden of his miss in 1991: 'There were two scenarios, you either put it over the bar and go four points up or else you go for it and try to kill the game. That would have put us six points up, and it would have been the first time that there was such a gulf between the teams so late in the game.' In his characteristic style of asking questions for himself to answer, he later recalled, 'I stood up and took the penalty and I missed the fucking thing! Did I see Mick Lyons running alongside me? No, I didn't. I believe I had the keeper beaten, but I didn't have the post beaten. Did it have any long-term effect on me? No it didn't. I didn't harp on it. Do I believe that the penalty stopped us winning the match? Yes, I do. I believe it was a major factor, if not the only factor in us not winning the match. But did it bother me? No, it didn't. I was disappointed, I was hurt. But that's life, you get on with it. To me it never affected me afterwards at all. Except,' he added with a laugh, 'that I didn't get a second opportunity to take a penalty!'

Back out in the US, lads from Roscommon, Galway, Westmeath and Silver Spring, Maryland, commiserated with me and it surprised me that I felt the loss keenly. Five weeks previously I had barely been aware that Dublin and Meath had drawn and now, on the far side of the world, I knew and I cared. I had needed to cross five time zones, but Dublin, Meath and Gaelic football had found me. When I had felt lost and alone in a foreign country, becoming a Gaelic football fan had been my way of connecting with other people. I had not seen any of the four matches, but, as a genuine – if new – supporter, the loss of the series twisted in my stomach. Not long afterwards I moved away from the family I first stayed with in the US and the pressure of two jobs and distance meant that I stopped turning up to football training and lost contact with the Irish and Irish-American lads. Yet, in two short summer months they had made an indelible impact upon me. I was one of tens – perhaps hundreds – of thousands who were brought to Gaelic football by the events of June and July 1991. That is why I understand what Jack Mahon (himself an All-Ireland medal winner with Galway in the 1950s) meant when, in describing the last game of the series, he wrote: 'It was Gaelic football's greatest day.'

Five

My Blue Heaven

THE WEEK BEFORE THE Leinster final in 1995 was all about Dublin and Meath. For the first time that summer, there were no other matches to be played on the same day. Consequently the newspapers were not required to split their attention. Acres of forests were culled to provide the paper for the countless words that were gushed forth to describe Dublin and Meath, Gaelic football's greatest show.

The years since 1991 had done little to separate the teams. Dublin had not played Meath in 1992, but had faced them in 1993 and 1994 and had beaten them by a single point on both occasions. In 1993, Jack Sheedy had exorcised the ghosts of his late, long-range miss in 1991. Dublin had been five points up early in the second half but Meath, as ever, clawed their way back into it, with Colm O'Rourke leading the charge. The tension in Croke Park could have been cut with a knife as Dublin struggled to keep their noses in front and Meath inexorably reeled us in. As the game went into injury time, Meath were a point down when a free was awarded to them a long way out. It seemed for a minute that there was some argument over who would take the free, with O'Rourke stuck in the middle of it. He walked away from the free-kick and back towards his marker, then turned quickly and the ball was chipped into his chest with his back to goal. Without ever needing to turn and locate the posts, O'Rourke slammed a long-range point over his shoulder and over the bar.

It was an extraordinary score. I and a couple of thousand other Dubs were mixed in amongst the Meath fans on the Canal End terrace and I could only shake my head in admiration of the cast-iron, ice-cold nerve of the man to even try such a shot at that stage of such a game. If it had gone wrong, all of Meath would have spent the next year castigating him for not trying to work the ball into a better position. He would have been accused of showboating, of not being a team player, of having an ego beyond his ability. But he had kept his head when all around him were losing theirs and had looked victory and defeat in the face and treated them both the same. He took the responsibility and he nailed it.

I turned to the Meath fan beside me and offered my hand. 'That point was something else,' I said. 'A draw is a fair result.' He looked down at my outstretched hand with contempt. As this was going on, Dublin won possession from the kick-out. Charlie Redmond went for a long-range shot but he was blocked and the ball squirmed to Jack Sheedy who, from 50 metres out, launched the ball into orbit. Sheedy was standing directly between me and the Hill 16 goal, so I knew the ball was going over the bar from the moment it left his boot. I turned to my contemptuous neighbour with both fists raised to my face and roared an ecstatic, wordless howl of delight and relief as the ball sailed over the bar. Then I, and all the other Dubs in Croke Park, danced and danced. The game was over, Dublin had won by a point and the beast had finally been vanquished.

I had returned from the US in 1991 with a desire to take a greater interest in Gaelic games, but it had taken me another year before I had come to understand the untamed magnificence that was Croke Park on a big match day. I was a supporter now, I swapped football stories with other guys and I felt for the Dubs, but I was used to watching sport on television and was relatively content to watch the Dubs play whenever the matches were broadcast. I wandered along to a live game or two in the 1992 season but it was not until the 1992–93 league final and its replay that I became really hooked. Dublin played Donegal in the league final that year, in a repeat of the previous year's All-Ireland final pairing. The matches were intensely dramatic – the first seeing two Dublin players sent off before it ended in a draw – and the raw passionate intensity from both sets of supporters was awesome. It is said that men have difficulty in expressing emotions, but in Croke Park men and women roared, cried, laughed, hated and loved with passion and abandon. It was intoxicating and I realised it was the only way to really experience being a fan.

Dublin did not play Meath in 1992 and so the 1993 Leinster final was my first face-to-face experience of the Meath supporters. It was not an experience I enjoyed. Not that there was any threat of physical violence, it was just that there was a tangible whiff of savage hatred from them. Meath's former captain, Liam Hayes, once wrote, 'They *are* crazy! Every last man, woman and child in Meath, at this time of year, views all of Dublin and the Dublin football team as a crowd of Serbs, or Iraqis . . . For some reason they view the blue shirt . . . as a direct threat to their own families and their forefathers who trod and worked the land of Meath. And that's the funny thing, because it is really the Meath supporters who are the more vociferous and hostile lot . . . They lose the run of themselves entirely and border on the lunatic.' Hayes was right. I knew Meath people, and knew them to be gentle, funny and decent souls, yet I could not reconcile that with the hostility of the Meath fans around me on the Canal End. The Meath fan who had stood beside me had fixed me with such a gaze of contempt when I offered him my hand that I could scarcely believe it. He was not a man blessed with handsome good looks and perhaps his manner was little more than an illustration of the old maxim that while beauty is only skin deep, ugly is rotten to the core. Nonetheless, I resolved to be elsewhere in Croke Park the next time Dublin played Meath.

The question was, where? On the Canal End the fans – Dubs and opposition fans alike – looked at the Hill 16 terrace at the far end of the pitch with a sense of awestruck trepidation. Even from the far end of the pitch, the wall of blue noise beat against your chest in waves and you could not help but be amazed that anyone came out of that churning sea of bodies alive. In the medieval world, mapmakers often filled in the unexplored margins of their maps with pictures of giant serpents and the annotation, 'Here be Monsters'. The Hill was like that unexplored world to many on the Canal End and they amused themselves with cautionary tales about the monsters that dwelled there.

'They'd piss in your pocket rather than go to the jacks and lose their spot,' said one.

'I hear the GAA spend a fortune on bleach up there after each game, 'cause they all just piss where they are standing,' said another.

'They're so busy beating the shite out of each other that they don't know who's won at the end of the match,' ventured a third.

The following year I watched Dublin against Meath in the Nally Stand, which shared the Railway End goal with Hill 16. The Nally Stand had reserved cheap seats for pensioners and students and lay beside the end of the Hill nearest to the goal. It was separated from the Hill by a heavy wire mesh that only furthered the impression that the Dublin fans needed to be caged. Indeed, the wild men among the Dublin fans behind the goal often seemed determined to reinforce this impression. From the Nally we could see them harassing the hapless Gardai who had drawn the short straw and ended up stationed behind the goal on the Hill. Regularly, sections of the Hill crowd would launch themselves at the bars of their cage and rattle the wire back and forth, making a sound like thunder, while roaring at the petrified pensioners and students on the Nally Stand only a metre away. Those sitting nearest to the Hill would occasionally be soaked with beer or cider as cans would be thrown from the Hill against the wire mesh. It seemed like only a matter of time before one of the pensioners would have a heart attack.

But, from the Nally, you could also see that it was only a small section of the Hill crowd that behaved like that. Down behind the goal they were mad but most were mad for what was happening on the pitch. Sure, some were drinking cider and others were smoking dope but, for the majority, the intoxicated look in their eyes was the result of events on the field. There seemed to be no pissing in pockets and few random acts of savagery. Towards the back of the terrace and further up away from the goal, the crowd was much like that on the Canal End, with one difference: here it was all blue. Three summers previously I had started to feel a sense of belonging and now, the closer I got to the Hill, the more I wanted to be there. I managed to get a Hill ticket for the All-Ireland final that year and took it with relish. In my excitement I took the wrong exit from the tunnel and ended up in the wildest part of the Hill among the mad throng that crowded directly behind the goal. I was in at the deep end and I loved it.

The Hill was a unique phenomenon in the world of Gaelic games. Typically different sets of supporters are mixed throughout the ground at matches. When Dublin were on the Hill, however, it became a culchie-free zone and anyone with the temerity to cheer for the opposition on the Hill would be greeted with abuse which would range from the good natured to the downright threatening. While many of those who travelled to matches from other counties were intimately involved in their own local club scene, some of us on the Hill barely knew where our local club was: our attachment was to the county side, not to a club. As a result, some Dublin fans were far less knowledgeable about the game than the corresponding fans of other counties. Not that this distracted us in any way from vocally offering our advice and abuse to both management and players. One time that the Dublin defender Ciaran Walsh was out of the starting team, he found himself on the Hill with a bunch of friends. Much to his surprise, five minutes into the game, someone near to him started to shout: 'Go on away out of that, Walsh, you are fucking useless.' It took him a moment to realise the abuse was in fact directed at the Dublin player on the pitch wearing the number two jersey and not at himself. His friends proceeded to strike up a conversation with the abusive fan, who continued to hurl insults at the player he thought was Walsh: 'You're a fucking moron, Walsh. You always were,' the fan roared and the group egged him on, asking him every few minutes how he thought Walsh was doing. It was midway into the second half when one of them told him, 'You know yer man Walsh that you've been giving out about? He's actually standing beside you.' Such stories were not untypical. There was a section of the Hill crowd who had never held a football in their hands but still felt entitled to abuse both players and managers from the terrace and on the national airwaves.

Yet for all that was wrong with it, the Hill was beautiful. On the Hill you never had to bite your tongue when you wanted to scream abuse at the referee or the opposition (or even your own team). On the Hill you never had to offer your hand to a Meath fan beside you (and have it refused). We could mix sociably with them before the game and afterwards but during the match the Hill cocooned us in a protective silk of blue and navy and kept us from getting close enough to offend the other. In the stands, mixed in with supporters of the opposition, it was harder to sing and keep singing because you were forever aware of their presence. The Hill was a release from normal obligations of civic decency and an opportunity to live viscerally. From now on, I would always be on the Hill.

Or so I thought. In the week before the Leinster final in 1995, tickets were not easy to come by and Hill tickets were surrounded with the elusive mystery of the Holy Grail. By the Tuesday before the game it looked as if the Hill ticket was a remote and receding possibility. I had an added problem in that I needed not one but two Hill tickets, because I had promised a French woman I knew that I would bring her to the match. It wasn't exactly a date as such – buried among the frenzied throng on Hill 16 was not, after all, the ideal first-date location – nonetheless I was still anxious to make a good impression. Sometime earlier in the summer I had been waxing lyrical to her about how one could never understand Irish culture without going to a Gaelic football match. (Why did I always talk about football when I met an attractive woman? Perhaps it was some sort of subconscious self-loathing, who knows?) She had responded that I would have to take her to a game and I had agreed. I had figured that Navan was not the place to introduce her to Irish culture – or, indeed, any sort of culture – and so I had promised to bring her to the Leinster final. Now the Leinster final was rapidly approaching and Hill tickets could not be had for love nor money.

Hill tickets were never easy to come by, but on this occasion the match was given an added significance by virtue of the fact that most of the major challengers for the All-Ireland had been taken out in their provincial championships. Donegal, Down and Derry, who had shared between them the titles of 1991, 1992, 1993 and 1994, were all gone in Ulster, and although Tyrone, the provincial winners in the north, were brashly promoting themselves as All-Ireland certainties, they were regarded as an average team with one superb player – Peter Canavan. Galway had triumphed in the west, but were thought to be unlikely to come through their semi-final against Tyrone. Cork had beaten Maurice Fitzgerald and Kerry in the south and posed the most likely real threat to the Leinster title winners. Cork had won two All-Irelands at the close of the previous decade and some of the great old warhorses from those campaigns were still playing. Kerry had looked competitive for much of the Munster final, but Cork had squeezed the life out of them with an undeniable ruthlessness. Still, Kerry had exposed enough Cork weaknesses to suggest that they could be beaten. All of this suggested that the winners between Dublin and Meath would be installed as favourites for the championship.

I spent all of Monday and Tuesday dialling the Dublin GAA county board, but the phone was engaged every time I rang. By lunchtime on Monday I had concluded that the phone was probably being left off the hook in order to avoid having to repeatedly tell callers that there were no tickets available. At the same time, I could not help but imagine a woman sitting in a bare office in an old red-brick Georgian townhouse with a pile of tickets beside her, stuffing a couple into an envelope each time she answered the phone. Every time I rang and the phone was engaged, I imagined her stuffing two more tickets into an envelope and the pile of tickets beside her dwindling ever smaller. By Tuesday afternoon I was frantic. It was at this point that I spotted a note at the end of an article on the sports pages. Tickets that had not been sold through GAA clubs throughout the country had been returned to Dublin and would go on sale at 9 a.m. on Wednesday morning. I would be there at 7 a.m.

I could scarcely believe my eyes when I turned the corner at 7.30 the following morning to see a queue of people snaking out of the door of the Dublin county board offices and down the street. A couple of people walked past me smiling with relief and holding match tickets.

'Are they already on sale?' I asked. Yes, I was told, the people in the county board had started selling them early because the queue was so long.

'Do they have many tickets?' I asked, anxiously. The guys looked back at the length of the queue and said that I would probably be all right.

'Do they have any Hill tickets?' I asked. The withering look I got required no answer. No, there were no Hill tickets to be had.

I half walked and half skipped along the length of the queue with giddy excitement and took my place at the back. The people there were telling each other what they knew, which was nothing.

'Your man up there says there's only a few tickets left and that we might as well go home,' one was saying.

'No, there's thousands of them left,' said another. 'Sure with the New Stand open they will be lucky to fill the place,' he concluded.

'You have your shite!' responded a third. 'This place will be packed to the rafters.'

I chipped in with what I knew, speaking authoritatively because my information had come from someone who had actually been inside. We should be all right, I told them.

'I hope so,' said one.

'We'd better be,' said another. 'I skipped my fucking breakfast for this.'

The line moved quite quickly and within 15 minutes I was inside the door. By then, we knew decisively that there were no Hill tickets to be had. Every person emerging through the door had repeated it as a mantra on their exit. 'No Hill'; 'No Hill.' Still, when I got to the table inside I had to ask, 'Do you have any for the Hill?' Of course not: no Hill. I took four Canal End tickets and was overwhelmed with a sense of relief. I knew now that I was going to the match. I skipped out the door, and even though they had been told before I felt compelled to explain why I was emerging with Canal tickets in my sweaty palm: 'No Hill,' I told them. Then I headed back up the street, trying to restrain the impulse to dance.

Thoughts of the Hill didn't end there, of course. There were rumours of a Hill ticket on the breeze. My mate Conor thought he could swing one, but it was elusive and, anyway, it was no use to me. I needed not one but two and there was no way I was going to get two. It was time to give up the dream and face the facts. I would be on the Canal End with three other people:

115

Conor (who was glad to have the ticket in the bag but had not yet given up the search for the holy grail of a Hill ticket), my French companion and another friend who was a neutral, from Limerick, but who never missed a match in Croke Park if he could help it.

We met in the Big Tree pub on Dorset Street about a mile from the famous old stadium on the morning of the match. The sun was blazing in the sky, as we had by now come to expect, and the pavement outside was packed with people in Dublin and Meath jerseys with some of the blue and white of Laois and the maroon of Westmeath sprinkled in among them. Laois, who had overcome Kildare in the underage semi-final replay, were to face Westmeath at 2.00 that afternoon with the throw-in for the main match happening at 3.45, and the last of the Laois and Westmeath fans were finishing their drinks before heading down to the ground. Outside the pub was a buzz of noise and excitement, as ticket touts wandered back and forth calling, 'Tickets . . . Any tickets . . . Buying or Selling . . .', competing to be heard with other vendors selling their wares: 'Hats and headbands . . . Get your hats, scarves and headbands . . .'

The Big Tree was a popular pub before a big game. They served food and so you could avoid the need to live off botulism burgers from a chip van by eating a decent Sunday lunch before heading to the match. Tickets were often available there and the bar staff would help people who had spare tickets to sell them on at their original price, thereby cutting out the hated touts who fed off our ticket-craving like vultures. The noise and the traffic of coloured jerseys back and forth ensured that even those with ice in their veins could not but be moved to excitement by the building colour and tension before the match. I did not have ice in my veins, but I did have the now familiar knot in my gut which was slowly but surely tightening with every passing minute.

Conor had not yet shown up and the remaining three of us sat having a drink in the cool, dark inside of the pub. All we could do was wait because there was no other way to contact him. In the summer of 1995 almost no one had a mobile phone, and texting was unheard of. Phones were expensive, with handsets alone costing around 200 Irish pounds (254 euro) and second-hand phones costing not much less. No one I knew really imagined a time when they would own a mobile phone, though pagers – which allowed people to leave a message which was then texted to the holder – were becoming increasingly popular. Conor didn't have a pager, however, so all we could do was sit and wait.

I had modified slightly the straw hat I had purchased before the Laois game with a needle and thread and now it looked like a genuine cowboy hat. The previous year's Dublin jersey and a pair of fake Ray-Ban sunglasses completed the effect. My French friend had dressed more conservatively and was nervous about being on a terrace surrounded by Meath fans. Surely fans should be segregated in order to prevent fighting and rioting, she had wondered. I had explained that fan violence was not really part of the GAA culture and that, while the mood may get tense on occasion, it would never get violent. Despite my reassurances she had chosen to wear neutral colours on the day. Now, seeing the Dublin and Meath fans mixing and drinking together, she felt a little embarrassed at her lack of faith in me and had bought herself a Dublin scarf to keep the sun off her neck. Nonetheless, I could tell she was still nervous.

Time ticked on and there was still no sign of Conor. The underage game was by now well under way and spaces were starting to appear in the pub as people began to leave to walk to the ground. Those without tickets were starting to get frantic now, and two teenagers wandered around and around the pub asking groups of drinkers if they had any spare tickets. They had already been to our table twice and been told no, but with no sign of Conor I was starting to think that maybe we did have one to spare.

'We're going to have to go soon,' my friend from Limerick said.

'I know,' I replied. 'Give him five more minutes.'

Then, suddenly, Conor appeared, leaning breathlessly on the side of our table, sweat glistening on his forehead. He was holding two pink tickets in his hand. 'Come on,' he said to me, with a glint in his eye, 'you have a Hill ticket.' I looked at him and then at my French friend, who was looking back at me with alarm in her eyes.

'I can't,' I said. 'I can't just leave people and go.' By 'people' I meant her. I was still hopeful that this first non–date might nonetheless go somewhere and, anyway, it wouldn't be fair to invite someone to a match and then abandon them to the Meath fans with only a total stranger for company. 'I just can't,' I said again and saw the relief in her eyes.

Conor looked around the table and then, with a half smile on his face, fixed his eyes on mine. 'Look,' he said. 'It's the Leinster final. It's Dublin against Meath. This is a Hill ticket. Now, am I going to give this away to some passing stranger?' There was a pause before I replied.

'You will have to,' I said with a sigh. 'I . . . can't . . .'

Conor stood up as one of the frantic teenagers was passing and called to him. 'You want a ticket?' he said. The teenager's face lit up, and, in that second, something inside me just snapped into place and I knew what I had to do. 'Wait,' I barked at Conor and turned to look at my French friend, who now had panic rising in her eyes. 'Look,' I said. 'I'm sorry about this and I only hope you understand later.' I gestured at my friend from Limerick. 'I promise you he's not an axe murderer and that he'll make sure you are all right. I'll meet you both back here later,' I told her. I handed my Canal ticket to the delighted teenager. Then I walked out the door to join Conor, who was standing in the sun grinning like the Cheshire Cat. 'I knew you wouldn't let me give away a Hill ticket like that. I just knew it.'

'I didn't,' I said.

'Ah, Ro,' he said, 'I knew.'

* * *

For the players, the week before Dublin played Meath was unbearably tense. Although they had beaten Meath the previous two years, this, in a sense, heightened the anxiety rather than caused it to abate. To beat Meath once was an achievement. To beat them twice was incredible. To plan to do it a third time was to plan for a miracle. At the same time, the management team had repeatedly emphasised to the players that they were in a position to give this Meath team a serious beating. Meath were, they told the players, in a hiatus, neither rebuilding nor still at their peak. 'I remember Pat O'Neill and Bobby Doyle in particular,' Keith Barr later said, 'for about three weeks continually emphasising that we were good enough to give them a hiding on the scoreboard.'

Dessie Farrell took that week off work, to get away from all the talk of the game. 'The hype is crazy for Meath games,' he said that week. 'Easily as much as for an All-Ireland final. The same with the pressure. The week seems to go very slowly.' He spent the week trying to get his game together, trying to get sharp. He took himself to the handball alley in St Brendan's Hospital and worked on his shooting and his first touch. Anyone who was available to bring the ball back was tapped up to help out, sometimes his sister, sometimes friends. He practised his kicking, aiming at an irregular spot high on the concrete wall of the alley. If he was accurate, the irregular concrete meant that the bounce of the ball was unpredictable and so his skills of gathering the ball were also sharpened. While the formal training of the team was wound down the week before the game, Dessie upped the tempo of his own private practice, wanting to wring every bit of his own ability out, wanting to be perfect for the match day.

For Ciaran Walsh, on the other hand, the week before the Meath game brought more disappointment. He had been sure that he had done enough in the Laois match to get back into the team. He knew that his first few minutes had been rocky and that Damien Delaney had been unlucky not to punish Dublin more harshly for his slips, but he had never wilted, had willed himself into the game and had taken control of his position and his man. He had not been fully fit or match sharp, he told himself, and the management would keep that in mind when judging his performance. With a game behind him and a few more weeks of fitness under his belt, he was certain he would be picked for the Meath game. But, when the team was announced on the Tuesday before the match, he was back on the bench, with Dermot Deasy back in the centre of defence and Keith Galvin retaining his position of corner-back. He was waiting once more.

For the players who were scheduled to play, it was hard to think about work, family or study while trapped in a goldfish bowl with the gaze of the nation and the weight of its expectation crushing down on you. Pressure for tickets was huge as some fans, in their single-minded pursuit of the elusive ticket, took to ringing players and their families in the hope of tracking one down. Unlike professional athletes, GAA stars were amateurs and had to work for a living: Charlie Redmond and Brian Stynes were firemen, like my father and brother (Stynes and my brother even worked in the same fire station), Ciaran Walsh worked in the same shopping centre as my mother, Mick Deegan owned a garage, and Dessie Farrell was a psychiatric nurse. Sixty-four thousand people would pay between six and twelve pounds for a ticket to see them play (much more if they needed to go to a tout) and all would roar themselves hoarse over their every move. Fifteen players would go home as heroes and fifteen more would go home broken, but none would go home having earned a penny. Because of this they were not, like professional athletes, locked in an unreal world away from the gaze of the public. They had to work, they were out there, they were exposed. The days ticked past until Sunday.

On the Saturday before the game, the team trained for the last time. They had a kickabout for half an hour, followed by a team talk, bringing them through tactics and cementing the work of the previous few weeks. Once more Pat O'Neill and Bobby Doyle focused in on the idea that Meath were there to be beaten, that this game did not have to be won by the odd point. It was an idea that was starting to sink in with the players.

Big match days had their own ritual for Dessie: get up and have breakfast; go to Mass; go for a spin on the bike to loosen the limbs; head towards Croke Park and make your way through the crowd milling around the stadium – all the time, trying to think positive and stay focused, all the time trying to fight the growing sense of desperation that this is the last chance: 'We have a feeling about us this season,' he said, that week. 'All the talk of last chances is over. We really know deep down that this is it, there'll be no rallying around next year. Fellas will retire, the new management will clear fellas out – might clear me out too. If we are ever going to do it as a team, this is the last chance.'

* * *

As we emerged from the tunnel under Hill 16 and into the sunlight, we marvelled at the massive new Cusack Stand that was being fully opened for the first time that day. The opening of what was still at the time called the New Stand marked the end of the first phase in the redevelopment that would see the old ground be transformed into the largest and most modern stadium in Britain and Ireland and one of the finest in the world. Parts of the New Stand had been opened for previous matches (I had watched the All-Ireland semi-final from its lower tier the previous year) but the Leinster final was the first time the whole stand was opened and it was magnificent. With two huge decks and a row of corporate boxes and ten-year seats between them, the new stand was enormous. The Hogan Stand that faced it was dwarfed in comparison. The New Stand was also beautiful. The huge spirals that ascended on its back and the distinctive wings of the roof became an instantly recognisable landmark that could be seen for miles around. Suddenly, it was clear that all previous stadiums in Ireland had never been anything more than glorified sheds.

The old stands in Croke Park had, in a way, symbolised the Ireland of the late 1980s and early 1990s. With their broken and dirtied panels which looked like nothing so much as the aftermath of a bad fire, their hard wooden benches and their toilets that would not have seemed out of place in the rough end of Calcutta, they epitomised the sense that the GAA and the country both believed that all their great days were now in the past. Ireland in the 1980s had sunk into an economic morass which everyone seemed powerless to correct. Unemployment was high, emigration was a way of life and Ireland's great monuments and great buildings were all the product of another age. Given that the GAA symbolised so much about Ireland, Croke Park could easily be taken as symbolising the decay at the heart of Ireland.

By the early and mid-1990s, sections of Irish society, including journalists on the *Sunday Independent* newspaper and *Hot Press* magazine who thought of themselves as being at the cutting edge of sophistication, saw the GAA, with its rural roots and its associations with nationalism, as being a symptom of what was wrong and backward with Ireland. Soccer, on the other hand, was seen as a symbol of what was good and forward-looking. However, the GAA, with one bold move, was about to turn the terms of this equation on its head and when, in 1995, Ireland's Celtic Tiger economy began to purr, it was Gaelic games – not soccer – that became the magnet for Ireland's newly wealthy consumers. As each new phase of the Croke Park development opened, more and more people flocked to see the stadium and to take in a game while they were there. The stadium also fitted neatly into the growing corporate entertainment market, and used corporate money to pay for 60 per cent of the cost in return for only 15 per cent of the seats. In the new prosperous and cosmopolitan Ireland, it was the GAA and its stadium which would be at the cutting edge.

We gazed at the New Stand for a few moments and then turned our attention to joining the rest of the lads at the back of the Hill. As impressive and meaningful as the new stand was, it was only concrete, glass, metal and plastic. The Hill may well have been far smaller but it was a human phenomenon and was therefore far more impressive than any mere architectural wonder. For the Dublin players, Croke Park was special and the fans throughout the ground were important, but it was the Hill that had an almost spiritual significance. Paul Clarke would later say, 'To see Hill 16 lighting up, the place where you stood as a young fella, all those people standing where you used to stand, to see that is amazing . . . Then you get your thoughts together and then the opposition comes out and the place lifts off again. The emotion is unbelievable. You try to keep your head down, but you have to have an old glimpse around the place. There's just this roaring noise and all the colour and you think, "This is it, this is what I play for."'

The Hill was a seething mass of blue and sound. The yellow-painted stairwells, which were supposed to be kept clear for emergency purposes, could not be seen under the crush of bodies. We pushed our way through the crowd and managed to join up with the rest of the lads towards the back. The sense of anticipation hung in the air along with the smell of other people's tobacco smoke. The sun was oppressive and on the open terrace there was nowhere to hide. No one today was laughing at the broad-brimmed cowboy hat that was stopping my face and neck from being burnt lobster pink. In front of us, there were dozens of men who had stripped to the waist and who were probably going to regret it when they sobered up. The lads were fidgeting anxiously, drawing deeply on their cigarettes, and someone asked who had bought a programme (the match programme, like the great big fuck-off-sized flag, was always desired and never purchased). I took mine out and it was folded open in order that we could once more look over the familiar names of our adversaries.

Robbie O'Malley (Publican): two All-Irelands, three National Leagues and three All-Star awards. Martin O'Connell (Meat Wholesaler): two All-Irelands, three National Leagues and three All-Star awards. Colm Coyle (Service Station Contractor): two All-Irelands and three National Leagues. P.J. Gillic (Panel Beater): two All-Irelands and three National Leagues. Brian Stafford (Company Representative): two All-Irelands, three National Leagues, three All-Star awards and Footballer of the Year 1987. Colm O'Rourke (Teacher, Journalist and Sport Shop Proprietor), now just weeks from his 38th birthday: two All-Irelands, three National Leagues, three All-Star awards and Footballer of the Year 1991. In the middle of the pitch, John McDermott was likely to win massive amounts of ball and unless Dublin could counter that, our forwards would be starved of possession. McDermott was an imposing figure, a big lean athletic man with clear ice-blue eyes that looked almost lifeless. In amongst these seasoned warhorses was a smattering of new young talent that we could not yet properly judge, including players like Graham Geraghty, Trevor Giles and Evan Kelly. 'Jesus,' someone whistled. 'These boys are one seriously mean bunch of fuckers.'

Sherlock had been picked in the full-forward position but it was expected that he would move into right corner-forward, where Colm Coyle would be marking him. Coyle had been puffing out his chest in the papers during the week and growling that Sherlock was 'welcome in his corner'. Regardless of the media hype, it was better not to put too much hope in Sherlock today, we figured. He was likely to spend a big part of the game with his hands to his face feeling blood drip through his fingers. On a more positive note, many of the other questions that had been asked of the Dublin team had been answered in the affirmative. Dessie Farrell had blossomed when he moved out into the half-forwards and was fast becoming a key playmaker. Paul Clarke had answered all questions asked of him too. At 191 cm (6 ft 3 in.) tall and 86 kg (190 lb), he was an imposing man with close-cropped brown hair prematurely flecked with grey. He had been tried in a number of positions in order to try to get the best out of him but in the last two games he had played with heart, brains and skill. Only the final half-forward position was now in doubt. Sean Cahill had not been named in the half-forwards on this occasion and the speculation was that Jim Gavin – the substitute who had provided the pass to Sherlock for his goal in the Laois game – would take his place. Dermot Deasy was back in defence and Paddy Moran would do as well on O'Rourke as anyone could, but whether or not Keith Galvin could hold his own against the powerfully built Tommy Dowd remained to be seen.

The bunch of lads that I watched matches with were the nicest bunch of lads you could hope to meet. A couple worked as volunteers, helping elderly people at the shrine in Lourdes. All were friendly, helpful, decent blokes with a sharp sense of wit. Until, that is, they pulled on a blue jersey and stood on a hillside above a grassy field with 13,000 other men and women in blue. Then they became rabid. They stood bolt upright, muscles straining and jaw locked as the terror that comes with being a football fan took hold. Veins bulged on the sides of their foreheads, and cords stood out on the sides of their necks and on mine too. Everything else was forgotten. The moment had arrived. The Dubs took the field.

'In the dressing-room area at the time, you could hear the crowd, from the moment they opened the door,' Dessie Farrell later told me. 'You might be seventh or tenth out, but from the minute the captain broke through the tunnel and came out the entrance the crowd would have got up. It was hair-raising stuff! It was a small, dark, tight tunnel, and even before you went out you were on edge. It was a great feeling though, a great sense of anticipation. You were anxious, but the adrenalin was pumping through your veins big-time. You needed to get out, get your first few breaths and get your hands on the ball. The burning desire was just to get out and get on with it, and, generally, you would almost take the door off the hinges trying to get out.'

The team's burning desire was matched by that of the crowd. The sound that emanates when your team takes the field comes from deep. It is not a shout, or a cheer, so much as a roar. It comes from the heart of your being and it contains all the anxiety, hope, fear and love that you have for the team taking the field. It twists your gut as you strain to find the breath to express all that you feel. All around you, grown men are roaring with the same passion, and, for a second, you are lost in a sea of noise, defenceless and protected in its midst. When it is over, the adrenalin pumps through every limb and your heart races as you raise your fists above your head in salute of your team and join in the communion of voices raised all around you, 'Come on you boys in blue, come on you boys in blue, come on you boys, come on you boys in blue . . .'

The pre-match ritual passed in a flurry of breathless anticipation. Both teams had burst onto the pitch in a frenzy of nervous energy and the old ground seemed like a bulging powder keg of tension. This was Sherlock's first experience of Croke Park with the senior team, something that would always have the potential to overpower a young and inexperienced player. As the players paraded around the pitch behind the band before the national anthem was played, Charlie and Mick Galvin spoke to Jayo, talking him through the pre-match nerves. Well they might, because there was a storm coming.

And when it came, it was a game to match the hype, a game that had everything. It exploded into life as if the referee had lit a fuse instead of throwing in a ball. Within seconds, both Sherlock and Keith Galvin were stretched out on the turf, holding their faces in agony, as Meath's grizzled old veterans sought to show them how hard it is to get on the ball when you are trying to pick up your teeth. The assault on Sherlock took place directly in front of the Hill, and the crowd were livid, venting their spleen at the Meath offender and at the unsighted referee in a cacophony of foul-mouthed abuse.

'Bastard. Fucking black-hearted vicious son-of-a-sheep-fucking-bog-hopping bastard,' shouted one of the lads while thousands more strung swear words together in equally inventive ways.

'There's ten thousand more behind you, you fuck,' the crowd warned the perpetrator.

The Meath fans, on the other hand, appeared ecstatic, having taken a particularly visceral dislike to Sherlock. Nothing gives rise to abhorrence so much as fear, and their loathing made it clear that they feared him. Both young players picked themselves up. They knew when they got up this morning that this would happen – we all did. It was the Meath way and it was never a question of 'if', only of 'when'. They knew it would happen and still they chose to be here. That was the measure of their courage and desire.

Immediately, it was Meath's John McDermott who demonstrated what a ball-winning threat he was to Dublin and within 15 seconds Meath were a point up. A fight erupted almost instantly as passions and pressure boiled over. The game continued but fists were flying all over the pitch as players sought to 'sort out' their opposite number. The journalist Paul Healy would later describe it as not being Gaelic football so much as 'fury with a ball'.

Dublin scored a couple of points before O'Rourke put over a free from an impossible angle to level things. Then slowly but inexorably Dublin took control. McDermott was having to follow his marker – Paul Bealin – out to the sideline, where he was winning no ball. Dessie Farrell was everywhere, snapping up loose ball in the middle of the field and setting up attack after attack with pinpoint passes. Sherlock was jinking and twisting back and forth across the field and, although he was not getting much ball, he was creating panic among the Meath full-back line and in his new marker, Colm Coyle, who no longer looked as confident as he had sounded during the week. Dublin went one up, then two. A hasty clearance from Coyle sent the ball over the sideline and from the resulting kick Dessie Farrell showed that it was not only O'Rourke who could kick points from an impossible angle. The Hill erupted, singing. Dublin were three clear.

But Meath, as ever, refused to lie down. Dessie picked up the ball again in the middle of the field and advanced towards the goal in front of the Hill. Dublin's forwards started to make runs to make themselves available when – BANG – Sherlock was stretched out once again, paying the price on the field for all of the attention that had been focused on him since the Laois game. Dessie coolly put the ball over the bar but the Hill was once more clamouring for blood, spitting streams of curses at Coyle and the referee, who seemed to have been unaware of the incident. The howls of the Hill and the gestures of the umpire finally alerted the referee to the episode and at last Coyle was booked for his efforts. Within a minute, the ball was raining back in on the Meath defence once more. Sherlock won the ball and shot for a point, but mis-hit the shot and it floated high in the sky before dropping once more infield. The Meath crowd erupted into laughter, baying like hyenas on amphetamines, delighted at the sight of Sherlock's error and no doubt hoping to dent his apparently inexhaustible self-confidence. Their laughter was stopped, however, as a Dublin player collected the loose ball. He seemed to be going nowhere, but managed nonetheless to scoop the ball out to Paul Clarke, wide in the corner. Clarke got a foot to the ball and neatly lifted it into Sherlock's arms and this time he made no mistake as he put it over the bar. As he ran back into position, he turned towards Colm Coyle and tapped a finger to his own chest as if to say 'That was me.' When half-time came, Dublin were leading by four.

Of course, four points was nothing. We had all seen this before. We wouldn't feel confident even if Dublin were six points up at this stage. Meath could not be demoralised, their will was too strong. They had not been winning the loose balls in the middle of the pitch, but we were sure that the time would come when they would. For the time being Dublin were muscling them off the ball, but that could not last.

Meath erupted in the second half and, within two minutes, had cut Dublin's lead to three. O'Rourke had become an irresistible force, smashing against the rock that was Paddy Moran who was having to foul him to stop him winning clean ball. A long ball was sent in the direction of O'Rourke and he and Moran strained muscle and sinew to reach it. It was O'Rourke that got the touch to it and deflected it into the path of the onrushing Trevor Giles, who let the ball loose to Tommy Dowd in front of the goal and suddenly it was 1991 all over again. This time it was Evan Kelly not Kevin Foley racing up the left-hand side, but the effect was the same. O'Leary came out to narrow Dowd's shot and Dowd moved the ball onto Kelly, who bundled it into the empty net. Meath were the classic ending to the horror story, the beast that just would not die. The Hill was shocked into confused silence and around the pitch the green and gold flags were being whipped back and forth in joyous celebration. Meath were level and the blood and adrenalin was coursing through their veins. They could smell victory and there were still 30 minutes to go.

But instead of dropping their heads and becoming disorganised, Dublin gritted their teeth and tore back into Meath with renewed ferocity. Both teams ripped into each other with an intensity that was hard to fathom. Although Meath now had the initiative,

Dublin's ferocity was such that Meath could not get the score that would put them in front and might psychologically crush the Dubs. The minutes ticked by. Finally, Meath got a point but it had taken eight minutes to come. Immediately, Paul Curran found Paul Clarke on the right wing and Clarke slotted the ball calmly over the bar to level the game again. Dublin, like Meath, would not lose this match. They would have to be beaten.

Dublin and Meath continued to tear into each other, but once more it was the Dublin players who seemed able to muscle their opposite number off the ball. Charlie pointed a free and Dublin were in front again. Suddenly, Charlie was everywhere. A few minutes previously he had missed a free, psyching himself out by convincing himself that the angle of a 21-metre kick was difficult. Now, driven by the belief that he had cost the team at a crucial time in the game, he was possessed by the desire to do something special to make up for the error. He later recalled, 'I received the ball 60 yards from goal and I turned inside a Meath player and crossed the 50. About halfway between the 50 and the 21-yard line Johnny McDermott was in front of me. I had to try to kick the ball over him, but my body position was all wrong and he started to drag me off my feet. As I was falling to my side I kicked it and when it went over the bar I couldn't believe it. Personally I think it was the best score I ever got.' It was a magnificent score and it lifted the fans and the team. Minutes later Charlie popped up again, this time in the right corner, sending an exquisite pinpoint pass to Paul Clarke, who put the ball over the bar when a goal seemed on. Dublin were three in front again and were choking the fight out of the gnarled Meath men.

Then came the moment that would continue to send a delicious shiver down my spine, even a decade later. Once more Meath had the ball and once more O'Rourke was the target. Moran and he arrived at the ball together and, although it looked for a second as if O'Rourke had it, with a gargantuan effort, Moran stripped the ball from his hands and it was punted to the middle of the field. Vinnie Murphy — who had recently replaced Mick Galvin — and Paul Clarke both went for the ball and it looked for a moment as if they might crash into each other, but Clarke left the ball to Murphy and set off to run the 70 metres towards goal. Meanwhile, Murphy shifted the ball to Sherlock, who had again lost his marker, and Jayo once more lofted the ball towards the posts. As the ball left Sherlock's boot, Dessie Farrell saw in his mind's eye the ball drop short, and shouted at Paul Clarke, urging him to keep running to be there for the dropping ball. From where I was at the far end of the pitch, it looked as if the ball was going over, but the braying laughter of the Meath fans on the Canal End let me know that, once more, it was dropping short. They should have learned their lesson the first time.

From the far end of the pitch it looked as if a scrum of players was waiting for Sherlock's ball to come down, although the television replays would later show that it was only two. But from 200 metres away there was no doubt that it was Paul Clarke's imposing frame that rose to meet the dropping ball, his right fist arcing upwards as if to dent the sky. He connected with the ball strongly and, in a flash, it was nestling in the back of the Meath net while the umpire beside the Canal End goal frantically waved the green flag to signal the score. Dublin were six points clear. The Hill erupted in a frenzy of noise and passion. The emotional weight of years of defeats to Meath was released as thousands of raw throats shouted for joy. We jumped up and down and I grabbed one of the lads and we hugged each other in a fierce embrace. We couldn't stop ourselves from jumping as we were buffeted through a maelstrom of emotions: joy at the goal, fear that it might not yet be enough, hatred for the opposition, pride in our team. Then the singing started and the giant choir raised their voices in their defiant hymn: 'Come on you boys in blue, come on you boys in blue, come on you boys, come on you boys in blue . . .'

There were 12 minutes left and the Meath fightback had to start again. Giles got a point for Meath, but immediately Paul Curran burst forward from defence and ran into space before nonchalantly slotting the ball over the bar. With that, we knew that, for once, there would be no fightback. Meath could not cope with the Dubs. They had thrown themselves against Dublin with all their might and had been broken. Dublin were on fire, playing football that they only ever dreamed they could play. Farrell knocked over a point. Minutes later, Jayo was dragged to the ground and a free was awarded. Enjoying himself by now, Sherlock trotted up to the referee, who was standing stiffly with his arm formally pointing towards the Canal End goal, and planted a delicate kiss on his cheek, an ironic thank you for the protection the referee had belatedly afforded him. Minutes later he swung over a second point of his own and the Meath fans were no longer jeering the shooting of our tough and sharp little corner-forward. Sherlock turned to the Hill and raised his arms in a victory salute. Well he might have, because this game was over.

Afterwards, my French friend smiled and said that, while she was angry at me when I walked out of the pub, the anger had faded once she came out of the tunnel beneath the Canal End, saw the Hill and felt the wall of noise as it rolled like thunder down the pitch. She understood then why I had to go (although we never did get to go on that date). I was still speechless at that stage, grinning from ear to ear in a mad and dizzy ecstasy. I could scarcely believe it. Dublin and Meath had played each other six times between 1991 and 1994. Three had been drawn and three had been won by a single point. The thought of a ten-point win was inconceivable but Dublin had been magnificent. That evening on television, one pundit said that Dublin had played the best football he had seen played in the previous ten years. They had been touched by the hand of the gods and had played like men possessed.

Back in the Dublin dressing-room, the jubilation was tinged with a sense of a job not yet complete. 'This is the sweetest day, I would say,' Paul Curran was telling Tom Humphries of the *Irish Times*. 'In all my years playing football, and there have been some fairly big games, this is the one that has given me most pleasure. Beating Meath by ten points after all the heartaches we have been through together.' At the same time, to this Dublin team, this was not a Leinster final, but an All-Ireland quarter-final. 'We have to go one step further,' Charlie was telling reporters. 'This is Meath but it is only a Leinster championship. If we go one step further this year, if we go all the way, it will make up for everything. Anything else won't.'

Six

Red-Eyed and Blue

BY THE BEGINNING OF August, it had become the most glorious summer I could remember. Sunshine was 30 per cent up on average, temperatures never seemed to drop below 20 degrees centigrade (68 degrees Fahrenheit) and, on occasion, sneaked up into the 30s (over 86 degrees Fahrenheit). Mid-July had seen a brief but torrential downpour of rain in Dublin that had been so severe that it had damaged roofs of shops and caused part of the ceiling of one cinema to cave in. Half of the rainfall normally expected in July fell in a few short hours. That phenomenal downpour was to be the last rain that Dubliners would see for a month. By August, the upper reservoir in Blessington that provides water for much of the south of the city had become a dry, cracked and baked expanse of earth into the centre of which some wag had stuck a 'No Swimming' sign. People were warned not to water their lawns or wash their cars for fear that water would have to be rationed, while in Northern Ireland fines were already being imposed upon those caught watering their lawns. The meteorological service began to cautiously hint that if the weather kept up, 1995 would be the hottest and driest summer in memory. Ireland was not alone in the heatwave it experienced that summer. The US, Britain and continental Europe also basked in blazing sunshine as weather records were broken throughout the northern hemisphere. Those who could remember pointed out that the Dubs had won the All-Ireland in 1983, 1977 and

1976, all of them notably good summers. It all seemed to make sense. Even the sky wanted to be blue.

As the hot, dry weeks of August passed, the excitement began to build as the semi-final approached and 'Jayo-fever' began to grip the country. After his performance in the Meath game, Jayo shifted from the back pages of the newspaper to the front pages and his profile now appeared under the heading 'National News' rather than only on the sports pages. The kid with the Asian features playing Gaelic football was the story of the summer. The Irish boy band Boyzone were topping the charts with their latest plastic pop confection 'So Good' and their manager, Louis Walsh, couldn't stop raving about Jayo: 'The guy has everything going for him, and the girls love him. He has star quality.' Jayo was on his way to becoming Gaelic games' first superstar.

Gaelic games were not designed to make superstars. There were many reasons for this. For one thing, the season was too short. While players in other sports tended to have nine months of the year to leach into the public consciousness, Gaelic footballers had at most four months per year. Secondly, the structure of the championship meant that half the players in the country were actually gone within a few weeks of the championship starting. While in other sports a star player can continue to try to impress even if his team is doing poorly, in Gaelic games one loss meant the end of the season. A player may build up a public profile one year and be knocked out in the first round of the championship the following year, never to be heard of again (as had happened to Down's Mickey Linden, the star of the 1994 season). In other sports a good player with a weak team will often transfer to a big club where his star quality can be shown at its best. But in Gaelic games, you represented your parish, your home and your county. The rules did not really promote player mobility (although sometimes they did move, as Larry Tompkins, first of Kildare and later of Cork, had shown). It was possible, therefore, that the best player in the country would be knocked out in the first round every year if he happened to be born in a weaker county.

Jayo did have some advantages compared with other players. Playing for Dublin meant playing for the most high-profile team in the country, the one everyone wanted to beat. His career as a professional soccer player in the League of Ireland (albeit with a small club) meant that he could pick up advertising sponsorship deals without it being immediately apparent that he was benefiting monetarily from his participation in the GAA (something that was not really open to other players at the time because of the organisation's strict policy on player amateurism). Yet the limitations inherent in the game were still there, and he overcame them. Peter Canavan, Charlie Redmond and Larry Tompkins were all better players than Jason but he had an X factor: good looks, boundless self-confidence and charm. RTÉ cut together a montage of some of his finer moments on the pitch and played it to the music of Dinah Washington singing, 'I'm mad about the boy'. And we were.

Jayo-mania was riding high on the wave of anticipation created by Dublin's ten-point demolition of Meath in the Leinster final. Even allowing for the fact that Meath had faded in the end, Dublin looked fitter, stronger, better organised and more intelligent in their play than any other team in the country. When Down and then Derry had crashed out of the championship early in the summer, the number of teams who might fancy their chances to beat Dublin was reduced substantially. With Meath now gone, many felt there were no other genuine contenders left. Dublin would win the All-Ireland, we were sure. All they needed to do was play like they did against Meath. All they needed to do was play like they had never played before.

The Dublin management were worried, however. Dublin had needed to reach a physical peak of fitness and a mental peak of preparedness to beat Meath. Yet there were still two months to go in the season. With a month between each remaining match, that peak of fitness would be almost impossible to maintain. Dublin had needed to peak to get past Meath but they had possibly peaked too early.

When the team turned up for training on the Tuesday after the Meath match, the management threw them a soccer ball and told them to have a bit of fun. They then retreated for a managerial meeting to sort out their plan for the next few weeks. Three players – Paul Curran and Mick Deegan in the half-backs and Dermot Deasy in the full-back line – had dropped below their target weight as a result of their training and the management decided that all three would be excused from training for the next two weeks in order to prevent their weight dropping any further because of over-exercise. Whether this would be enough to maintain the required fitness remained to be seen.

* * *

It is said that one used to be able to tell which side a family was on in the Irish Civil War by looking at the newspaper they bought. Those who bought the *Irish Independent* were generally on the pro-treaty side, while those that bought the *Irish Press* were more than likely anti-treaty. (The *Irish Times*, although nominally a national paper, was, historically, not widely available outside Dublin while the *Cork Examiner* was a phenomenon of that county and it was widely accepted that the normal rules did not apply down there.) When I was a kid my family did not buy a morning paper but the evening paper that we had delivered was the *Evening Herald,* a stablemate of the *Independent*. On both my mother's and father's sides of the family, there was a clear antipathy to Fianna Fáil and the cultural milieu from which it sprang. This antipathy spread to, and included, the *Press* group of newspapers.

Yet the cultural milieu of the *Press* included Gaelic games, and it seemed that one could not properly be a Gaelic football fan unless one read the *Press*. I had taken to getting the *Evening Press* as I headed for the bus home in the evenings, and to wrestling with the large, broadsheet pages as I sought to make my way through the relevant sections without assaulting the person crammed into the seat beside me on the bus. In truth, the only bit of the *Press* I was really interested in reading was the sports column of Con Houlihan. Houlihan was a legendary character in Dublin at the time and there were many evenings when my friends and I would sit in Mulligan's Bar on Poolbeg Street behind the Press building, watching people walk up to Con to ask him a question or two, just to be able to tell people that they had spoken to the legendary Con Houlihan. Born, as he wrote himself, in the hills above the town of Castle Island, County Kerry, in 1925, his weather-creased face and his bedraggled grey hair made him a postcard image of 'the man from the west'. He once described himself in these terms: 'Con Houlihan, stage Kerryman, B.A. (pass), great lover (failed), an enthusiastic cook who, as far as is known, hasn't poisoned anybody yet, turfcutter (retired), journalist (kind of), rugby player (a long time ago).' When writing, he combined his love of rural pursuits and Kerry ways with a prodigious knowledge of art and literature and a creativity without parallel. Writing in a newspaper brings its own shackles on style. It does not allow for long paragraphs or winding phrases. Houlihan wrote clever and engaging prose in short paragraphs and shorter sentences, and became the undisputed master of his craft. With him, every article seemed like a journey. An article may start with the weekend's game and end up as an appreciation of the poetry of Gerard Manley Hopkins, yet this leap would be achieved with a fluency and ease that made it seem not only sensible but actually necessary. Equally, a preview of a big match might begin with an evocation of a forgotten autumn and the look of the mist across the landscape as one cycled the last 50 miles to Dublin to see a long-past All-Ireland final. Houlihan became a character in his own story, he wove himself in and out of his articles and readers felt that they had come to know him, a warm-hearted, engaging – and surreal – old friend. He came to feel like that to me too, and, though I never wandered over to speak to him, I enjoyed the companionship of his words as I read and the bus trundled me home.

As well as a broad grasp of literature and a capacity for heart-aching descriptions of landscape, Houlihan was known as the master of the simile and the metaphor. Some of his descriptions were unforgettable and were often recited by fans years later as they sought to make a point or win an argument. Twenty-five years after the event, one of my colleagues used to regularly evoke Con's account of how Mikey Sheehy lobbed the stranded Dublin goalkeeper Paddy Cullen in the 1978 All-Ireland final: 'And while all this was going on, Mike Sheehy was running up to take the kick – and suddenly Paddy dashed back towards his goal like a woman who smells a cake burning. The ball won the race and it curled inside the near post as Paddy crashed into the outside of the net and lay against it like a fireman who has returned home to find his station ablaze.'

Houlihan's brilliance was more than just in his descriptive capacity. He was also an astute reader of the game and his columns often interpreted for people games they had themselves seen and thought they understood. The journalist Eamonn Sweeney tells of an occasion when, as a youngster, he had asked an elderly man who was reading the *Evening Press* what he had thought of the game. 'Whist. How do I know what I think until I've finished reading what Con has to say?' the old man replied. In any argument on any game, citing Con's view was regarded as a definitive.

The 1995 season, however, passed without the *Irish Press* as a guide. In May, on the same day that I had injured my back, the *Irish Press* newspaper lurched into a crisis which led to the next day's newspaper failing to appear. Since industrial relations crises were no strangers to the *Irish Press*, most people assumed that this crisis was just another problem which would blow over. That was not to be the case. The *Irish Press* was already dead, it just didn't know it yet. Its final agonies would last the summer.

The disappearance of the *Press* sparked an enormous public response. People may not have been reading the *Press* in massive numbers anymore, but they cared for it, like an old friend they saw infrequently. The journalists began to produce a strike edition of the *Press*, called the *XPress*, which was sold for one penny (always with the option of a larger contribution) on the streets around Liberty Hall and O'Connell Street in Dublin. It seemed everyone wanted to support the striking workers. Jack Charlton and the Irish soccer team turned up to support them; Nobel Prize winner Seamus Heaney read poetry to raise funds for them; filmmaker Neil Jordan ran a movie screening and lecture on their behalf; leading actors of stage and screen organised a benefit gig; and U2 gave an exclusive interview to the *XPress* in order to help raise funds. The *XPress* became a focal point for Dublin's cultural life during that long hot summer, and I went out of my way to get a copy every day. *Press* journalists and writers provided colour pieces and interviews that kept interest in their plight and their writing alive. Con Houlihan was at his very best, recounting his life story over multiple issues in his own unmistakable style.

But, while the city and country seemed to be willing the *Press* back to its feet, the vultures were gathering. Spotting a gap in the market, the English newspaper *The Sun* doubled its distribution to the Irish market and slashed its price. The week before Dublin played Louth, the *Press* management made the decision to liquidate the company, a decision which gave rise to further bitter court battles that raged on through the summer. The *Press* journalists continued to produce the *XPress* in the hope that some other investor might be found to save the paper. In the weeks before Dublin played Cork in August, an examiner was appointed to try to save the struggling company. Some thought it was the last chance for the paper, but others thought of it as akin to rearranging the deckchairs on the *Titanic*.

* * *

With two weeks to go before the match, the Dublin squad started to play football again at training sessions, and Curran, Deasy and Deegan once more began to take an active part in training. The Dublin management remained worried about the mental and physical state of the side, however. Dublin had been raring for an opportunity to have a go at Meath, but facing Cork did not have the same acrid tang as a match against Meath. Once more, the focus turned to the possibility that this Dublin side could go down in history as 'the nearly men', and the management emphasised that they still needed to atone for past failures. At the same time, there was a growing fear that the team might be going stale and losing their sharpness. Although many in Dublin and in the (Dublin-based) national press thought that Dublin were now a cast-iron certainty for the All-Ireland title, the squad seemed edgy and nervous.

Cork, on the other hand, seemed relaxed and confident in the week before the semi-final and certainly did not think of themselves as out of the running. They came to the game with some serious footballers and some crucial experience and no one embodied those two characteristics better than their great import, Larry Tompkins.

Perhaps the match that best characterised Tompkins was the All-Ireland final of 1990. There had been 14 minutes to go in that match when Tompkins, Cork's captain, collided heavily with Meath's All-Star defender Martin O'Connell in front of the Hogan Stand. The collision had ripped at Tompkins' cruciate ligament and severely damaged it. He was already on painkilling injections to allow him to play despite a calf injury and had previously damaged the medial ligaments in the same knee, so, as he got to his feet, the leg had wobbled beneath him, the ligaments that held his lower leg to his upper almost all shot. Pain had coursed through every cell in his body. Staying on the pitch had seemed impossible.

Cork had, two weeks earlier, won the hurling All-Ireland and if they went on to win the football as well in the same year they would have achieved an incredible feat. Cork were, at the time, reigning All-Ireland football champions, but Meath had beaten them in the All-Ireland finals of 1987 and 1988, muscling in and intimidating Cork with their indomitable will. The matches between Cork and Meath had been marked by the level of aggression between the teams which had grown to become an intense bitterness between both sets of players. This had been the first time the two had met in championship football since those two matches. Beating Meath would not only have meant a second All-Ireland in a row for Cork, and a historic football and hurling double, but would also have symbolised that Cork had not only matched Meath's skill but also their savage determination. It would be a triumph of will, all the more so because Cork had played much of the match with a numerical disadvantage after referee Paddy Russell had sent off a Cork player. Tompkins stayed on the field and Cork won their place in history.

But Tompkins was about more than just determination. He was also an extremely skilful footballer who could run with the ball, find teammates with pinpoint passes or else simply score himself. As Keith Barr later recalled, 'He was a phenomenal footballer, a total footballer. Larry Tompkins could play wing-forward, centre-forward, midfield, anywhere. He could kick points, score goals, take free-kicks, he was phenomenal.' His prematurely balding head gave him the look of a player who had more years under his belt than was actually the case. No one should have been fooled by his appearance into believing he was a has-been.

In addition to Tompkins, Cork also had experienced players like Niall Cahalane and Danny Culloty. Cahalane was Cork's captain, a teak-tough and determined defender who could also drive forward to supplement the attack. He was, above all else, the beating heart of the Cork team, the man who would set the example which other players would strive to match. Midfield was manned by Danny Culloty, who had learned to play Gaelic football in Golden Gate Park while growing up in San Francisco. He and Liam Honohan were regarded by many as the best midfield pairing in the country. Cork were managed by Billy Morgan, the Cork goalkeeper and captain from the '70s. He was a proud and thoughtful man, whose teams were almost invariably strong, skilful and committed.

To this group had been added quite a few players who were hungry to emulate the feats of previous great Cork teams. Mark Farr and Mark O'Connor completed the full-back line along with Cahalane. O'Connor had been peripherally involved in a furore two years previously which to some showed how editorial standards in the *Press* group were slipping. The morning after Derry had beaten Cork in the 1993 All-Ireland final, an article appeared in the *Press* under the byline of Alison O'Connor which described, amongst other things, how the author had spent the night before the match sharing a room with one of the Cork players. Some readers may have thought this helped to explain Cork's performance on the day of the final but a correction published subsequently made it clear that there was no sexual implication to the article; rather the words attributed to Alison in the article should actually have been attributed to her brother, Mark. O'Connor was a tall and strong player who was likely to be marking Jason Sherlock. Just after the Meath game there had been a media flurry when O'Connor had been quoted as making various statements about Jayo that he subsequently dismissed as tabloid fabrications. O'Connor was a good player who had been improving throughout the championship and was fast as well as strong. It was entirely possible that he would have the speed as well as the strength to tame the boy wonder.

At the far end of the pitch, Colin Corkery was Cork's free-kick specialist and was coming into the game with a total of thirty points scored so far in the championship, seven more than Charlie Redmond. Like the rest of the Cork forward line, he was strong and capable. In short, Cork had strength in all areas of the pitch, from defence to attack, but were particularly strong around the middle third of the field. Just like Dublin, they had watched throughout the summer as many of the leading contenders for All-Ireland glory had slipped by the wayside. Also like Dublin, they had demons to exorcise.

Following their two All-Ireland victories at the end of the '80s, Cork had, like everyone else, been broken by the victorious Ulster teams of the early and mid-'90s. In 1993, Cork were back in the All-Ireland final, this time against Derry, who had defeated Dublin by a point in the semi-final. Niall Cahalane had come into the game with an injury, had been wearing a special cast and had needed several painkilling injections before taking the field. Derry figured that Cahalane's injury would make him the weak link in the side and so subjected him to intense physical punishment. His shoulder ligaments got torn away after one collision. Then he lost two teeth in another. He got hit from all sides, on and off the ball. He needed at least four painkilling injections at half-time to be able to come out for the second half. Cahalane played poorly and Cork lost by three points. He later recalled, 'It was a terrible day. The only time in my life that I have wanted to walk away from football.' The defeat in the 1993 final was followed by a semi-final defeat to Down in 1994. So 1995 was to be their third All-Ireland semi-final in a row and on each of the two previous occasions the team that had beaten them had won the title. Those defeats stuck in the gullet of the Cork team and burned in their collective chest. As with Dublin, only an All-Ireland victory would silence the ghosts that now haunted them.

* * *

By August, Dublin was abuzz with football fever. For once, I was not frantically searching for a ticket, as my brother had got a Hill ticket from his workmate Brian Stynes, the Dublin midfielder, and he had passed it on to me. Of course, by now I really should have had a fix on a final ticket or at least have started the process of digging one out but that trail was still cold. In 1993 I had got two final tickets from the father of my then girlfriend, but she and I had parted ways and subsequent girlfriends had not been in a position to furnish tickets so readily. In 1994 I had got a ticket at the last minute from my friend Conor, but, since the Leinster final, work had taken him away to Germany. I had gone to the well so often at this stage in search of tickets that I had drained it dry. Where my All-Ireland ticket was going to come from was a mystery and one that was bothering me already, but for the time being I could do nothing but relax and soak in the atmosphere that pervaded the city.

Suddenly, I had no difficulty in finding people to talk to about football in Dublin's pubs. The large number of people around Dublin from Cork or with Cork links also meant there was plenty of opportunity to engage in banter with the Cork crowd. Dublin and Cork have always had a very special relationship. Dublin may have been the legal capital of Ireland but Cork was said (by Cork people) to be the 'real' capital of Ireland. It had, they liked to tell us, the country's tallest building and it had an Opera House (which Dublin did not). Whatever you had, Cork had one bigger or older, cheaper or better. If Dublin caught a cold, Cork, you could be sure, had double pneumonia with a twist of tuberculosis. Like the English, it was said that Cork people considered themselves a self-made race, thus relieving God of a terrible responsibility. Not all Cork people were like that, of course, but there were enough to ensure that you could usually find a few that could be easily baited if you knew how to get at them. It was not only the Dubs who enjoyed using Cork people's sense of superiority to wind them up; in fact, it could be described as something of a national pastime. There is a story told of a GAA congress at which a Cork delegate made a passionate speech which ended with the pronouncement, 'I was born a Corkman, I live a Corkman and I'll die a Corkman.' The Kerry delegate who was next to speak began by remarking that it was typical of a Corkman to show such a lack of ambition.

Being something of an anorak, I had spent the previous few years gathering stories of Dublin football lore and, on the day before the game, my stock of tales was added to by the papers which carried accounts of prior meetings between the two teams. Of these prior meetings, the matches of 1974 and 1983 were deemed by Dubs to be the most significant. That evening I got my chance to bring some of these tales into play as I found myself sitting with a group that included two Cork people in the laneway beside Toner's Bar on Baggott Street, smoking and drinking while the sound of the Outhere Brothers singing 'Boom, Boom, Boom' blasted from a nearby car stereo. It was a balmy summer evening and I sought to entertain the group by drawing the indignation of the Cork couple.

Of all the meetings between the teams, I told the assembled group, the 1974 All-Ireland semi-final was a match that could truly claim to have changed the history of the GAA. Despite a chorus of jeers, I continued and pointed out that this was the day that the Cork football team actually became the midwives that facilitated the birth of the phenomenon known as 'the Dubs'. When All-Ireland champions Cork turned up to play Dublin in the 1974 semi-final they expected to waltz past these new upstarts into the final. Dublin were a second-division team that had somehow managed to win the Leinster title, but although they seemed to have a growing momentum behind them, those who knew Gaelic football were far from sanguine about their chances. Billy Morgan's team were an excellent side that included players like the legendary hurling and football star Jimmy Barry Murphy. Leaving their hotel to go to the match that Sunday, some of the Cork supporters were so supremely confident of victory in the semi-final that they booked their room for the All-Ireland final. One Cork fan put into words what many people felt when interviewed for a newspaper the day before the final: 'Cork are scientific footballers,' he said, 'and Dublin are a shower of mullickers. The case will be proven on Sunday.'

Sunday came, and Dublin blew Cork away.

The victory over Cork in 1974 was more than just another football match, however: it was in this moment that 'the Dubs' were born. After the Leinster final of 1974, a number of new phenomena had started to become evident in GAA circles. Firstly, a new word was introduced to Ireland's vocabulary: the 'Dub'. Prior to 1974 the term 'Dub' was only used by one Dub to describe another. By the time of the Leinster final that year, the term was on everybody's lips. Newspapers started to refer to 'the Dubs', putting the phrase in quotation marks at first in order to emphasise that it was a phrase with which they were unfamiliar, but it quickly became an accepted part of the vocabulary. Along with 'the Dubs' came a wave of colour the like of which Irish sport had never before seen. Dublin's distinctive strip of a sky-blue shirt with navy shorts was introduced for the first time in 1974 (prior to that they had worn sky-blue jerseys and white shorts) and the colour scheme became an immediate hit. Dublin's footballers' success brought ever-growing crowds of new fans to Gaelic football: 37,000 for the Leinster final and 42,000 for the All-Ireland semi-final. It became apparent that Dublin was a sleeping giant, waiting for a sporting phenomenon to capture the mood and the attention of the city. The Gaelic football team became that phenomenon.

The birth of 'the Dubs' was about more than just numbers, however. Prior to the emergence of the Dubs, football attendances were largely grey in colour as people went to Gaelic football matches wearing their Sunday-best suits. The Dubs on the other hand were influenced by the soccer they watched on television and turned out in blue and navy, carrying banners and singing football anthems. Two-tone hats made of crêpe paper and cardboard which could be bought on the way to the match and which were just about sturdy enough to last till the final whistle were the standard issue. If it rained, the dye would run out of the hat and the wearer would make their way home with blue and navy streaks running down their face, but that was an occupational hazard many were willing to risk.

Although Hill 16 had been associated with Dublin football in the '50s and the '60s, the Dubs of 1974 made the Hill the preserve of Dublin fans as never before. In the same way that Liverpool was famous for its Kop terrace and Manchester was famous for its Stretford End, the Dubs on Hill 16 became, from 1974 onwards, a phenomenon to match any other in world sport. On match day the Hill would became a swaying wall of blue and navy, a rolling sea of bodies and noise carrying a hundred banners which proclaimed that 'The Jacks are back', 'Dubs Forever', 'Heffo's Heroes', or 'Heffo's Army'. Had Cork managed to live up to their billing in 1974, I continued, the history of Irish sport may well have been quite different. Many of Dublin's new-found fans were uneducated in the ways of Gaelic football because the game had never before caught their attention. The Dubs of 1974 had done just that. The numbers of Dublin football fans rose and rose during that season, but the growing fan base was, initially at least, based on the team's success. Had the team fallen somewhere along the line then it is likely that much, if not most, of the new-found supporters would also have drifted away with nothing more than fond memories of one crazy summer. Cork did not match their billing, however, and Dublin fans were given the opportunity to grow knowledgeable about the game and became a part of it. More than that, many of the Dublin team of 1974 were already long in the tooth and the great Jimmy Keaveney had already retired once before making a comeback in that season. Had they been beaten that day it is possible that they would have faded away once more, but Cork's failure to defeat them gave them the chance to go on to become one of the greatest Gaelic football teams of all time.

As a coda, I also pointed out that Cork had also provided Dublin with the ultimate opportunity to show that they were as good away from Croke Park as they were in the capital. In 1983, Dublin met Cork once more in the All-Ireland semi-final and were lucky to get a second chance at Cork, who had been five points up with only nine minutes remaining and had still been three clear with only thirty seconds to go. Then Dublin's Barney Rock got free of his marker for the first time that day and blasted the ball into the back of the Cork net. It was regarded by many as the best game of football seen since the classic semi-final of 1977. The replay was scheduled to take place the following week and Dublin agreed to the match being played in Cork rather than at Croke Park. The GAA then decided that the game would not be televised in case it drew attendances away from other matches that were being played around the country on the same day, a decision which gave rise to a huge commotion. Given the economic hardship of the time, many traditional Dublin supporters were not able to afford the trip to Cork and the failure to televise the game meant they would not see it. Of course, many throughout the country pointed out that it cost as much to go from Cork to Dublin for a match as it cost to go from Dublin to Cork and that it was about time that the Dubs were required to see what it cost the rest of the country to get to matches in Dublin. Some supporters in Cork chuckled quietly to themselves. Getting Dublin outside Croke Park and away from their massive support could only, many believed, increase Cork's chances of beating the Dubs. But the Dubs turned out in massive numbers for the game, turning Cork's grim and forbidding stadium into a sea of blue and navy, and, on the pitch, the Dubs mercilessly overpowered a shell-shocked Cork side by 4–15 to 2–10.

All of this was good material but, ultimately, it was not all one-way traffic. Indeed, the only game against Cork which mattered by the mid-1990s was the 1989 semi-final, when Cork had struck two goals to claw back a seven-point deficit in the first half and gone on to win by four points. Keith Barr had been sent off that day after being goaded into retaliation. One of the two Cork people sitting outside Toner's Bar that evening had been at that game (or at least claimed to have been at it), and so he promptly retaliated to my stories with his own account of 1989 before finishing by noting that those who cited ancient history were usually those who had nothing recent to crow about. That shut me up.

I met the lads early on the day of the match in the Liffey Bar beside Liberty Hall and had a bite of lunch and a cup of tea. I made it a policy never to have more than one pint before going to a match, particularly if I was going to be on the Hill, since the crush of the crowd meant that getting to the toilet was near to impossible. The city was abuzz with the upcoming match. Crowds wandered up and down O'Connell Street in the blazing sun, with the blue and navy of the Dubs clashing everywhere with Cork's red and white. I clutched my ticket in an envelope in my jeans pocket and kept my hand on it just so I would know it was still there. I could feel the envelope getting damp in my pocket as the sweat from my hand transferred onto the paper, but I didn't care. My heart was in my throat already. I didn't need any further excuse for anxiety.

Cork is known as the 'rebel county' and their supporters carried confederate flags from the US Civil War, as well as Japanese flags, Ferrari flags and anything else in red and white that could be found. Cars honked good-naturedly as gangs of people milled across the traffic lanes of Dublin's main thoroughfare and air horn buzzers rent the air. We walked up O'Connell Street and past Barry's Hotel, which was always crammed with Cork people when they made it to Dublin for a match. The crowds there were all in red and white and had spilled out onto the street from the bar inside. 'Come on the fucking Rebels!' someone shouted every time a bunch of Dubs walked past. 'Jaysus, it's a long way to come to take a beating, lads,' one of the

Dubs called to the crowd as he walked past and they responded with catcalls and the blast of an air horn. 'It must be great to have an excuse to get out of Cork all the same,' called another on the way past.

In the late 1980s, Cork people had started to get lazy about making the trip to Dublin for the semi-final, since they had gotten used to the idea that they should save their money and spend it when they got to the final, but those days were now past and the Cork crowd had turned out in numbers. Once inside the stadium, the atmosphere was electric. At one end of the old grey ground, the Hill was drenched in blue and in full voice. A huge television screen had been installed at the back of the Hill in order to give the crowds in the Hogan and New stands and on the Canal End a better view of the proceedings. Much to the chagrin of ticket-hungry Dubs, this resulted in the capacity of the Hill being reduced by about 3,000, but this did not affect the thunderous noise which emanated from the terrace, as the Dublin fans sang 'Molly Malone', followed by 'Come on you boys in blue', hyping themselves up for the entrance of their team. Many of the flags on the Hill carried Jayo's name, and it looked like the boy wonder had been adopted by the Hill as our icon. At the other end, the Cork fans on the Canal End were also in full voice and had brought a wealth of colour and excitement to match that of the Dubs. With the opening of the New Stand, the capacity of the ground had increased and in excess of 64,000 people had squeezed into the old cathedral of Gaelic games and they were making themselves heard halfway across the Irish Sea.

The Dublin team erupted onto the pitch first, to be met by the characteristic roar of the crowd. Both teams warmed up for a while, the intensity of their exercise routines making clear to all that both were focused on the next 70 minutes as the most important minutes of their lives. Charlie, Keith Barr and John O'Leary gathered together in a huddle in front of the Hill goal and shared the moment with each other. The teams then both lined up behind the band for the traditional parade around the pitch. The parade started at the halfway line near the Hogan Stand and made its way up to the Canal End first, and as it passed the crowd went wild, waving flags, honking air horns and roaring 'Come on Cork', or 'Come on the Dubs', each in line with his or her own persuasion. It traversed the length of the Canal End and along the New Stand, before stopping at the halfway line once more and turning across the pitch without coming near the Hill. For a number of years opposing teams had been showing their fear of the Hill by breaking away from the parade before it reached our end. Now it seemed the authorities were legitimating their fears by not asking them to parade in front of the Hill. The Dublin team broke away from the shortened parade and made their way down to the Hill to receive a rapturous reception and fans and players stood and applauded each other. Then the referee, Pat McEneaney, called the two teams together and prepared to start the game. He checked with his linesmen, P.J. Quinn from Down and Paddy Russell. They both signalled that all was well. He threw in the ball and the game was on.

When the game came, it was almost an anticlimax and should have set alarm bells ringing in advance of September's final. For 20 minutes, Cork managed to maintain the pretence that they believed they could win the game. For that 20 minutes, the fans on Hill 16 felt the gnawing pangs of anguish and worry. Cork started like a thunderbolt. Within seconds of the opening whistle, the ball was fired into Cork corner-forward Mark O'Sullivan, who darted out in front of Keith Galvin to reach it before being unceremoniously dragged and pulled in front of the posts. Colin Corkery, Cork's methodical free-kicking answer to Charlie Redmond, scored the resultant free and Cork were in front.

Dublin were clearly worried about the power of the Cork midfield and as a result were dropping balls short of midfield for the half-backs to collect and set up attacks. Every Cork man seemed to be faster to the ball, however, and Dublin were having to give away free-kicks which were inevitably resulting in scores for Corkery. Only Charlie's free-kicking was keeping Dublin in the game and he landed two long-range frees to keep Dublin in touch. Cork were leading by two points at the 20-minute mark when the signs began to get ominous for Dublin. A ball was sent in towards Sherlock directly in front of the goal. It was at the perfect height for him and he started a metre in front of his marker, Mark O'Connor. It seemed for a moment that a Dublin goal was potentially on the cards, but O'Connor powered past Sherlock, brushing him out of the way like a charging bull faced with a rag doll. The crowd on the Canal End erupted in joyous celebration at seeing Dublin's great hope being dismissed with such casual ferocity, and their cheers grew louder still when the ball immediately found its way to Mark O'Sullivan, who again escaped Keith Galvin to score a good point at the other end. Throughout the pitch, Dublin players were being beaten to the ball by their markers. The midfield could not seem to win any ball. It seemed as if the vibes that had been emerging from the respective camps during the week were accurate: Cork were relaxed and full of confidence while Dublin were edgy and nervous. The Dublin team's mood began to spread to the Hill, which was also now getting nervous and quiet.

Then, in a moment, everything changed. Often one spends time after a match trying to identify when things changed and generally it is impossible to find a single defining moment. Change is usually a gradual process, the result of a series of minor modifications in positioning or tactics that tilt the balance one way or another. Here, however, the match changed as if someone had flipped a switch. Cork should have won the free-kick in the middle of the field as Stynes was, without a doubt, pulling Danny Culloty to the ground while the San Franciscan leapt to try to claim the ball. But the referee saw it differently and blew up for a free-kick for Dublin. Keith Barr later recalled, 'The Cork goalkeeper kicked it out. I was marking Tompkins, and myself and Tompkins were going for the ball and I nudged or pushed – however you want to put it – I fouled Tompkins going for the ball, but there was a foul before that and I think that's what the referee blew up for. The ball landed in my hands and I felt it was a free for Cork. Now, I was near the Cork half-forward line, well out of position. So I pretended not to notice that it was a free for Cork. I thought to myself "Don't look at the referee, keep the ball and release it quickly." At least if the referee blew up again and gave the free to them, I would still have had time to get back into position. So, I saw Sherlock move and I put the ball in, out in front of him.' As the Cork players turned towards the referee as if to complain, Keith Barr launched the ball towards the corner, allowing Jayo plenty of opportunity to get out in front of O'Connor. He did. Jayo collected the ball 20 metres out from goal, but O'Connor stayed with him well and was now positioned between him and the goal. There seemed to be no real danger for Cork. Sherlock faked as if to go to the left, then the right. Then came the moment that changed everything. O'Connor slipped.

With a single bound, Jayo was loose. He breezed past the stricken defender with thoughts of a goal filling his mind. O'Connor lunged at him despairingly as he went past, the anguish of his error etched on his face. For years afterwards, Mark O'Connor would be haunted by this image as a major chain of bookmakers turned the photograph of that moment into an advertisement that was prominently displayed in its shops' windows nationwide. Every time he passed a shop from that chain, O'Connor would have seen the photo of Jayo speeding towards goal with his own face in the background, torment written across it, watching Sherlock vanish out of reach. Jayo lost the ball for a moment on

155

the solo and that took him wide of the goal but he had time to gather it again. From a very acute angle, he let fly and buried the ball past the diving keeper and into the far bottom corner of the net. Then he wheeled away, arms spread wide to accept the acclaim of the Dubs behind the Canal End goal, before nonchalantly jogging back into position. The crowd erupted, singing 'BOOM, BOOM, BOOM, let me hear you say Jayo, Jayo!' The Outhere Brothers had never sounded so good and the summer had a new anthem.

The goal punctured Cork's confidence and resolve like a balloon that has been in collision with a truck. It was as if a hypnotised man suddenly woke up and found himself on a high wire above the Grand Canyon, gripped by terror and by the realisation that he was not a tightrope walker after all. Once the goal celebrations had died down the Dublin fans began to sing at the Cork crowd, 'You're not singing, you're not singing, you're not singing anymore!' An injury to Paul Bealin meant that Cork had time to regroup their thoughts but it did them no good. They had the next scoring opportunity but fluffed it. Now the crowd were singing 'What the fucking, what the fucking, what the fucking hell was that?' Charlie Redmond had no such nerves, however, when the ball next came to him, and, in the space of three minutes, Dublin went from three points down to one point up. 'Easy! Easy!' chanted the Hill. When the ball was next kicked into the middle of the park, it was Brian Stynes who leapt and won it unopposed. He moved the ball to Paul Clarke who passed it to Mick Galvin who was, in turn, dragged back by a floundering Cork captain, Niall Cahalane. When the free-kick was awarded, Cahalane became a hurricane of rage, berating Pat McEneaney, the referee, then the umpires, shouting like a man possessed at all about him for their failure to see whatever slight he had imagined had led him to fouling Galvin. 'Wake fucking up, Pat! Wake the fuck up!' he spat through clenched teeth. In response, McEneaney penalised his dissent by moving the free-kick closer to the goal. Cahalane continued to fume as Charlie sent the free over the bar but it was not the referee or the umpire he was really angry at; rather, it was the Fates who had written this role for him. His rage was like that of a man as he fell from a high building, watching helplessly as the ground below – and the end of his journey – grew ever closer. Dublin scored 1–3 in the second quarter of the game, with Cork responding with a solitary point in injury time, Mark O'Sullivan getting away from Keith Galvin as he had on almost every other occasion that the ball came their way. At half-time Dublin were leading by two points.

It shouldn't have been all over but, in the stands and terraces, most people were sure that it was. There was no doubt that Cork should have been able to make up the two-point deficit. They had, after all, done much the same against Kerry in the Munster final, but Dublin were not Kerry and were not going to be overpowered by Cork. Cork's best chance had been to blind the giant while it slept, but Jayo's goal had raised the Dubs from their slumber. Cork would fight back but Dublin would be ready.

Ciaran Walsh had watched the first half from his spot in the dugout, directly behind manager Pat O'Neill. He had been gutted when, the Tuesday before, the Dublin management had taken him aside and told him he would be starting the match as a substitute once more. Keith Galvin had, however, experienced a torrid first half, with Mark O'Sullivan losing him at will. Still, the management decided to make no change at half-time and gave Galvin five more minutes to show what he was capable of doing. Walsh emerged from the tunnel after half-time with the rest of the team but took his place on the bench behind O'Neill.

When the second half began, there was, initially, no Cork fightback. It was Dublin who played as if they were behind, straining muscle and sinew to reach every ball and to make every tackle. Drenched in sweat under the unforgiving sun, they ran as if they could feel nothing but a cool evening breeze on their backs, supported each other and always ensured that the man with the ball had someone to pass to. When Cork had the ball, Dublin got men around them, making it impossible for them to make headway. One Cork attack was ground down until the attacker was reduced to firing a hopeful pass towards the front of the Dublin goal, where it was picked up by Mick Deegan.

Six metres from his own goal, Deegan set in train what was later to be dubbed the score of the season. He passed the ball back to John O'Leary, who in turn passed it to Stynes, who had by now covered every inch of grass on the pitch. Stynes carried the ball forward before moving it to Dessie Farrell, who shifted it on to Mick Deegan, who had moved up to the 45-metre line, before he found Paul Curran in space. The fluency of Dublin's passing meant Cork could not get near the ball. Curran accelerated away from his marker before lofting the ball towards Mick Galvin, who had left Cahalane flailing in his wake. Galvin passed it crisply to Paul Clarke, who was by now raiding up along the wing under the Hogan Stand. From a tight angle, Clarke stroked the ball sweetly and it dropped over the bar. Dublin were easing away from Cork now and the crowd were singing once more: 'BOOM, BOOM, BOOM, let me hear you say Jayo, Jayo!'

At last, the Cork fightback came, and from a familiar source. Cahalane won a ball in the Cork defence and, his face locked in a ferocious scowl, brought it out into midfield before it found its way to Larry Tompkins. Tompkins looked up, saw no Cork player giving him an option, and decided to go for it himself, launching the ball high into the air where the wind helped to carry it over the bar from 45 metres out. The Cork crowd were lifted momentarily and when their team scored another point it looked for a moment as if they were fighting their way back into the game. Keith Galvin lost Mark O'Sullivan three times in the move which led to Cork's second point of the half and O'Sullivan had been clear on goal when the player in possession had opted instead to take the point. The Dublin management decided it was time to put Galvin out of his misery, and, seven minutes into the second half, he was substituted. For Ciaran Walsh the long wait was over. He bounded onto the field like a coiled spring being released and his arrival was greeted with a huge roar of approval (and relief) by the fans. A point from Mick Galvin edged Dublin four points clear again and threw a fire blanket over the Cork revival. There were still 25 minutes to go, but the game was dying.

Cork scored a couple of points but Dublin responded with a brace of their own, Mick Galvin bringing his total to four points. Against Meath, Dublin had pushed on to destroy their opponents. Maybe they had physically passed their best by August, or maybe they simply did not fear Cork like they had feared Meath, but here they seemed content to allow Cork, who, with the exception of Tompkins and Cahalane, seemed to lack the belief that they could win, to bob along within four or five points of them. Ciaran Walsh stuck to O'Sullivan for seven minutes before Cork managed to send a ball in their direction. It was the moment that Walsh had been focused on since the Laois match a month and a half earlier. He flew out in front of O'Sullivan like a greyhound released from the traps and won the ball with O'Sullivan trailing in his wake as the crowd roared their approval. He knew in that moment that he was back. O'Sullivan barely touched the ball for the remainder of the game.

Cork had scored points by the bucketload in their earlier championship games, but had not scored a single championship goal all season and never created a clear-cut chance here either. With ten minutes to go the Cork crowd were streaming out of the gates in the hope of getting on the road back south before the rest of the traffic, and the Hill, once silenced, was raising its voice in renditions of 'You're not singing anymore' and 'Cheerio, Cheerio, Cheerio'. For a brief moment, those leaving their seats stopped and looked as Tompkins set off on a run half the length of the pitch. Keith Barr later recalled, 'I remember Tompkins getting the ball around midfield and he started a run, but I backed off him and backed off him. Tompkins was the kind of player who could score a point comfortably from 50 or 55 yards. I kept backing off him, but when he didn't kick the ball from 40 yards, I knew he was going for goal and once he got into the 30-yard zone I fouled him. I knew he was going for a goal or trying to create a goal, because they needed a goal to get back into the game. The foul gave us an opportunity to get numbers back and forced Cork to kick the ball over the bar.' Barr was content to surrender a free and take a booking, but determined that never again would Dublin lose to a late goal. Cork scored two late points to come within a goal of Dublin, but it was a goal that they never looked like scoring. Cork were like a swimmer that had plunged into a torrent and swam with vigour for a few moments only to discover that his limbs had tired before the current did and so was swept away.

Midway though the second half, Charlie Redmond had got involved in a minor altercation with Cork's Mark Farr. A few minutes later, Farr punched Charlie in the back and Charlie reacted rashly, flashing out his hand and making contact with Farr's face. It could have resulted in a sending-off, but the referee was content to issue a warning. While some players might have played up the incident in the hope of getting Charlie sent off, to Farr's credit, he sought to intervene with the referee on Redmond's behalf. Given what was to happen less than a month later, the warning signs should perhaps have been spotted, but were not. As the final whistle went, Charlie ran to Farr, embraced him and said his few quiet words of apology before the crowd streamed onto the pitch and engulfed him. Down in front of the Hill, Jayo had enough time to swap jerseys with a Cork player before he was hoisted aloft on the shoulders of a crowd composed mainly of teenage girls and carried away, with a broad grin on his face. The crowd were ecstatic and in love with Jayo, who had punctured Cork's self-belief with his goal. But all the tumult, noise and exhilaration could not hide the fact that this was Dublin's poorest display in the championship so far. Those with calm heads looked on from the emptying terrace and wondered if they should worry. Dublin had beaten Cork, and semi-finals were all about winning, but the manner of the victory had to raise concerns. For the first 20 minutes, Dublin had been like a rabbit caught in a car's headlights. Although Jayo's goal had sparked them into life, when they had got ahead they had lacked the ruthless resolve to finish off their opponents that they had shown against Meath, while Charlie Redmond's flash of temper had been potentially costly. For anyone looking to read the tea leaves and see the future, all the signs of what was to come were there.

* * *

The following morning the courts heard that attempts to find an investor for the *Irish Press* had been finally stymied by what the court-appointed examiner called the 'difficult attitude of the shareholders'. The game was finally up and the *Press* group slid quietly into history.

Seven

North Country Blues

WHEN I WAS A school kid, the end of August was always the end of the summer. The days were getting noticeably shorter by then and the summer that had once looked like it was going to last forever was now unravelling with ever-increasing speed as school once more loomed into view and hurtled towards us. The beginning of September meant a new uniform, new classrooms and teachers, another year passing and the excited chatter of the summer's news.

At the end of August 1995, the weather finally broke and Irish skies darkened once more with the once-familiar sight of rain clouds. Our long hot holiday at home was nearing an end. But the business of the summer was not quite over yet. Over 30 counties had started out in the championship in May. Over half were gone within a few weeks. By the time the season was half over at the end of July, only four teams remained. Now, heading into the last month of the championship, there were only two.

Dublin had started four months previously with a cloud of questions hanging over them. They had not had a settled group of forwards that were proven scorers. People wondered if the players who had withstood such emotional and physical wear and tear over the previous five years could galvanise themselves for one last tilt at the title. Now, having reached their third All-Ireland final in four years, only one question remained: did they have the will that was needed to finally take the title?

Their opponents were to be Tyrone, the dark horse of the championship. When, at the beginning of the season, team managers had been surveyed as to who would win the All-Ireland, not one had thought to mention Tyrone as a possibility. Newspaper articles that appeared at the outset of the campaign had neither mentioned Tyrone as possible winners nor even as pretenders whose claims to the title would ultimately be found to be unsubstantiated: they were simply not on anybody's radar. Like Dublin, they had reached the All-Ireland final without fully answering the questions that people felt hung over them. They had, some felt, too many small and light players to be genuine contenders for the All-Ireland. It was also said that the team had too many ordinary players in both attack and defence to be seriously considered. Apart from one blistering half a game of football, when thirteen Tyrone players had defeated Derry, their season had in fact been the story of one extraordinary footballer, Peter Canavan. And that was the biggest question which now hung over Tyrone: could one man really win an All-Ireland on his own?

'The All-Ireland final is now a matter of nerves,' Brian Mullins, Dublin's star midfielder of the '70s and '80s, had said on television immediately after Dublin beat Cork. 'This Dublin team should, maybe, have two or three All-Irelands in the bag already. There will be very little done on the training field that will improve fitness between this and the All-Ireland final. It's all psychology now.' Mullins had won four All-Irelands and knew what it took to win one but, as in politics, a week can be a long time in sport, and a month can be a lifetime. No one at that stage could really have predicted the events that would lead to the 1995 All-Ireland final being one of the strangest, most controversial and most memorable ever.

* * *

At the west Tipperary home of Paddy Russell, the postman dropped the news through the letterbox. 'We are pleased to inform you . . .' the letter from the GAA head offices in Croke

Park began. It was not entirely unexpected. Paddy had already that year refereed the national final of the club championship, the National League final and the Munster final between Cork and Kerry. It was clear to all that he was a referee at the very top of his trade. The fact that there was no Munster team in the final had improved his chances even further but, still, being asked to referee the All-Ireland final was a big honour, one that never came to most referees. For Paddy Russell it had now come a second time. Having refereed the 1990 final between Cork and Meath, he was now to be the man in the middle for the Dublin and Tyrone final of 1995.

Soon, the telephone began to ring. Once the name of the All-Ireland referee had been announced, the media throughout the country, hungry for All-Ireland football news to fill the sports pages and satisfy the craving public, wanted to know something about the man who would stand in the middle. He got calls at work and at home. One northern newspaper wanted to know his favourite food, his favourite drink and the person he would most like to meet in the entire world. In an interview with the *Irish Times* he spoke about his wish to remain as anonymous as possible during the big game. 'Paddy Russell is the referee for the senior final and he will be the happiest man in Ireland if he is ignored even more after the match is ended,' said the article. 'It is the sincere wish of every referee who ever blew a whistle that his contribution to the occasion not be the subject of debate or, at most, that it be regarded as peripheral or insignificant.' Unfortunately for Paddy Russell, that was not going to be the case and events on All-Ireland Sunday would plunge him into a maelstrom of comment and would ensure that his role in the final, far from being anonymous, would never be forgotten.

* * *

The last week in August and the first weeks in September seemed to me to drag by. The summer had been filled with football, with intense emotions rising to an almighty crescendo, but now the pause button had been pressed and everything was on hold. In the newspapers, the space that had been filled with football was now filled with other sports, as if the world had forgotten that there was still one game left to play.

But thoughts of Gaelic football were not far from my mind, even when late August brought the news of the death of Jackie Carey, arguably the greatest Irish soccer player of all time. Carey had played for Manchester United between 1937 and 1953 and had been voted British Footballer of the Year in 1949 and British Sportsman of the Year in 1950. Matt Busby, Manchester United's legendary manager, had listed him alongside the greatest of all Manchester United players and regarded him as a better player than Bobby Charlton, Denis Law or George Best, because Carey could play in any position, including goal. The papers also alluded to Carey's background in Gaelic football: he had been picked to play for the Dublin Junior team at the age of 16; however, the rules of the GAA at the time had meant that any player found to be also playing 'foreign' sports was banned, and, as a result of being caught playing soccer, Carey was lost to Dublin GAA. He wasn't the only player lost to the GAA in this way. His contemporary, Con Martin, had played Gaelic football with the Dublin team that won the provincial championship in 1942, but, before that year's All-Ireland final, a spy from the GAA's Vigilantes Committee had spotted him playing soccer and he had been expelled from the GAA. His provincial winner's medal was withheld from him, and when Dublin won the All-Ireland that year for the first time in 19 years, Martin was not allowed to play. He later went on to play soccer for Leeds United and for the Republic of Ireland, and was one of the goalscorers in 1949 when Ireland became the first team from outside the UK to beat England on their home soil (Jackie Carey was the captain of that Irish team). Despite all he achieved as a soccer player, Martin listed his lost All-Ireland as one of the great regrets of his sporting life.

The death of Jackie Carey brought these stories to the fore, and also brought up questions about the way in which nationalism and the GAA went hand in hand. The 'ban' (as the prohibition on 'foreign' sports was called) had been removed in the early 1970s, and there were plenty of examples of later exchanges between Gaelic football and other sports. Kevin Moran, who won two All-Ireland medals with Dublin in the 1970s, had gone on to a soccer career with teams such as Manchester United and Blackburn Rovers. In late 1994 there had been frantic rumours that Moran was to return to Gaelic football and play one more season with Dublin in 1995 before finally retiring. The rumour was probably just a joke (though it excited much discussion at the time) but there was no question that the fans would have welcomed him with open arms. Niall Quinn had also gone from Gaelic games (in his case, hurling) to a career in English soccer. Yet, despite these later examples, the legacy of the ban was still felt into the mid-1990s, particularly for people of my father's generation. For many of them, their formative years had left them with the view that the GAA was a small-minded organisation that worked to impose its games upon people rather than develop in people a love for them. Indeed, the fact that GAA rules in the mid-1990s prohibited games perceived as being British games from being played in Croke Park (while leaving it open for American football and for rock bands) was, for them, further evidence that the GAA's brand of Irish nationalism was nothing more than anti-British prejudice.

As the debate raged, it inevitably moved into discussing the differences between what the GAA meant in Northern Ireland and what it meant to us in the south. Some felt that, given the suffering of many of the nationalist population in Northern Ireland, they were, in a sense, more fully Irish than us in the south who had long had it easy and, consequently, had lost touch with the suffering which defined what it really meant to be Irish. By the early 1990s the loyalist paramilitaries were killing more people each year than the IRA and, although some of these killings targeted known members of the IRA or Sinn Fein, the majority were simply ordinary Catholics murdered while going about their daily business. In the North, the links between the GAA and nationalist politics meant that it could generally be taken for granted that someone playing Gaelic football or hurling was a Catholic. Loyalist paramilitaries therefore needed only to track down someone on their way to or from football or hurling training in order to be reasonably sure of finding a Catholic to kill. Many of those who played football or hurling north of the border were forced to vary their routine as they travelled to and from training or matches in order to avoid making themselves an easy target. Among the many with GAA connections murdered was Sean Fox, a 72-year-old pensioner who had no connection with Sinn Fein or the IRA and who was interrogated and murdered in October 1993 by loyalist paramilitaries. He was honorary president of his local GAA club.

Nor was it only the loyalist paramilitaries who used the GAA as a means of identifying people. The British army and the police tended to regard the GAA as part of an alliance of forces that was antagonistic to their state and often treated it accordingly. In Crossmaglen, south Armagh, the Gaelic football pitch was taken over by the British army to use as a helicopter landing pad. Those going to Gaelic football matches were often harassed and held up at checkpoints so long that they couldn't reach the game on time. In February 1988, 24-year-old Aidan McAnespie was on his way to a local Gaelic football game when he was shot dead as he walked through a British army checkpoint. Officially his killing was described as an accident, but his family believed that he had been killed deliberately, citing a history of harassment and verbal abuse directed at the dead young man by soldiers.

The GAA, for its part, did little to reach out the hand of friendship to the British security forces. The GAA's Rule 21 meant that members of the British security forces were banned from membership of the GAA. While the bulk of Northern GAA members (like the bulk of Northern Catholics) did not support the IRA, many IRA members adhered to the cultural nationalist ethos and, as such, were GAA members or supporters. Seamus Harvey was goalkeeper for Crossmaglen Rangers Gaelic football team until, while on active service with the IRA, he was shot dead in an SAS ambush in 1977. In the IRA sections of the Maze prison, inmates organised mini-Gaelic football matches between prison wings or between the different counties represented. Given this, it was hardly surprising then that many Protestants in Northern Ireland did not see themselves in a position to take an interest in Gaelic football. In fact the GAA conspicuously sought to associate itself with political and cultural nationalism in Northern Ireland. It was, as the Derry journalist Nell McCafferty once said, part of nationalists' cultural resistance.

All of this meant that the GAA meant something different north of the border than in the south and, in a sense, this tension between north and south ran through the heart of the GAA. North of the border the GAA was still part of the cultural resistance against British occupation, yet south of the border a number of the lads I went to matches with played cricket as well as Gaelic football. North of the border many GAA people regarded the British army, the police and prison officers as a force of occupation to be resisted, yet Mick Deegan, Dublin's star wing-back in 1995, played soccer with the Northern Irish club Crusaders where one of his teammates was a prison officer from the Maze prison. The GAA was caught between these two views of itself. Many Northern members sometimes felt that the GAA marginalised them and did not sufficiently support their struggle. At the same time, many GAA people in the south felt embarrassed by the way in which the GAA mixed sport with an anti-British political agenda that not all GAA members shared. Others in the south made repeated reference to the hardships suffered by GAA members in the North and suggested that there still remained good reasons for the anti–British political agenda.

This debate rumbled on against the backdrop of a political landscape in Northern Ireland that was darkening once more. The early 1990s had seen some of the worst political violence in 20 years in the North. The same day on which Dublin drew with Kildare in the first round of the 1994 football season, six people had been murdered in the Heights Bar in the quiet, tiny village of Loughinisland, County Down. The 1994 season lasted long enough to see the declaration of the IRA ceasefire at the end of August and this was followed within six weeks by the declaration of a ceasefire by loyalist paramilitaries. The preparations for the 1995 All-Ireland finals were, therefore, taking place against the backdrop of the first anniversary of the ceasefires in Northern Ireland and as television adverts identified the need for peace to be built, saying, 'Wouldn't it be great if it were like this all the time?' But the events of the summer had soured the sense of hope. The week before Dublin had played Laois, riots had erupted in Belfast after the British government had released a British soldier who had been convicted of murdering a teenage Catholic girl. That same weekend, rioting also broke out at Drumcree church while nearby the Reverend Ian Paisley told marchers, 'If we don't win this battle all is lost. It is a matter of life or death. It is a matter of Ulster or Irish Republic. It is a matter of freedom or slavery.' In the first week in September, while claiming to be on ceasefire, the IRA murdered Tony Kane, a suspected drug dealer, as he sat in his jeep outside the funeral service of his aunt.

In the days before the final, one Ulster Unionist councillor complained about British government money being spent on an advertisement in the final's match programme because the advert contained three words in the Irish language (the advert also contained over 130 words in English). Yet, at the same time, there were also signs of a thaw in the air. The Royal Black Preceptory, which was linked to the Orange Order, informally allowed Tyrone Gaelic football flags to be hung from what remained of their ceremonial arches, while the Ulster Unionist MP John Taylor, who had once been shot in the head by the IRA and survived, had no hesitation in wishing the Tyrone team every success over Dublin. As a consequence, our conversations and arguments about the 'ban', about Rule 21 and about what it meant to be Irish were all carried on with a sense that things were changing and that hope was possible. We did not know at the time that these fragile hopes for peace would be smashed the following February when the IRA would end its ceasefire by detonating a massive bomb in London's Docklands, killing 29-year-old Inan Ul-haq Bashir and his friend John Jeffries as they worked in a newspaper kiosk.

* * *

While the fans were searching for something to fill their time in late August and early September, the players also found that time began to drag. After the match against Cork, the Dublin team returned to training on the following Tuesday with their numbers depleted once more by those who had to catch up on time lost at work and those who needed to rest their sore bodies. The difficult task now facing Pat O'Neill and his management team was to plan the next three weeks to keep everyone fit and focused for the final. This task was made all the more difficult by the fact that the Dublin team, unlike their opponents, were living in the capital and the home of the national media. Journalists, desperate to catch a player and get a quote before he went to work, took to ringing players at home at 7.30 in the morning. The media pressure got so intense that some players took to leaving their phone off the hook. A storm of controversy developed when Jason Sherlock suggested to a journalist that he should contact Sherlock's agent in order to see about an interview. It was suggested that he was trying to sell an interview and in doing so to breach the amateur ethos of the GAA. In fact, all Jason had wanted was some respite from the never-ending barrage of pressure, but some journalists scurried to create stories and controversy where there were none.

Everywhere Sherlock looked, he met his name or his photograph. In the days before the final a series of adverts appeared selling sports shoes by proclaiming, 'Jason Sherlock scores in his bare feet. The rest of us need a little help.' His shoeless strike against Laois, like his goal against Cork, had become the stuff of legend. He had become public property and everyone wanted a slice.

Work was no respite for any of the players, since strangers would wander in off the street to check if a player was fit and uninjured, to wish him well and, sometimes, to see if the player could rustle up a ticket for the final. Charities and other good causes made contact through friends and relations to see if a player could attend a launch or provide a photo opportunity. Everyone meant well, but retaining focus became increasingly difficult while living in a goldfish bowl.

Passing spare time became a chore, something that started to take on mammoth proportions. Players watched themselves carefully at training so as not to pick up an injury, knowing all the time that an ankle can be twisted as easily on the stairs at home as on the football pitch. Gardening was avoided in case someone accidentally stuck a pitchfork through his own foot. Some took to standing a metre back from the kettle as it boiled in case they ended up accidentally scalding themselves. They knew it was stupid, but couldn't help themselves. Every movement, every moment was now looked at through the lens of the third Sunday in September.

As the weeks slipped away so did the sharpness that comes from playing championship football. The players had been ready for the final the Sunday after the semi-final, but the championship calendar dictated that they must wait for a month. They struggled to stay fit without straining themselves, to stay alert without exhausting themselves, to satisfy the demands of a craving public without losing sight of the fact that it was all about the match. September could not pass quickly enough.

* * *

Tyrone travelled to the final as underdogs. They were a team that was small in stature, something that gave a considerable disadvantage in the physical world of Gaelic football. While ten of Dublin's starting fifteen weighed in at over 82 kg (180 lb), only four of the Tyrone team were of a similar size. Although Tyrone had the tallest and heaviest player on the pitch in goalkeeper Finbar McConnell (98 kg in weight and 193 cm tall – 216 lb and 6 ft 4 in.) and Dublin had the smallest and lightest in Jason Sherlock, these two were the exceptions on their respective teams. Nor were Tyrone an experienced side at the highest level. While most Tyrone players had won medals at underage and university levels, none had previously won anything in the senior championship. While Dublin had five players in their team who had previously won All-Star awards, Tyrone had only one. Indeed, the only Tyrone player who was widely known outside Tyrone was that player, Peter Canavan.

At 24 years of age, Canavan was reaching his peak as a player. He looked physically unsuited to the game of Gaelic football. At 175 cm (5 ft 9 in.), he was relatively small for a footballer (he was the same height as Jason Sherlock), and at 73 kg (161 lb), he was lighter than any player on the Dublin team except Sherlock. With a prematurely balding head and lacking the square-jawed visage common in many footballers, he looked like the sort of player who could be physically dominated out of the game. But looks were deceptive. There is a story told about an occasion when Canavan was still a schoolboy and was playing against a Cork team in a national schools' championship. The Cork team had heard about this dangerous player called Canavan, but had no idea what he looked like. When the Cork side spotted a diminutive player on the pitch who was wearing a substitute's jersey but was playing nonetheless, they assumed that he was a substitute who had been called late into the game due to an injury to a starting player. They ignored him while trying to figure out which of the rest was the player they should be keeping an eye on. By the time they had worked out that the small kid in the sub's jersey was Canavan, he had destroyed them.

Canavan was an extraordinarily gifted footballer. While most other players could kick well only with one foot, he could kick accurately off both left and right feet. Typically a defender would try to shepherd a player onto his weaker foot in order to limit attacking options. With Canavan that was not an option. He was a nippy player, perhaps not the fastest around but with great acceleration and phenomenal balance that enabled him to get out in front of his marker and to twist and turn and create space for himself. He was comfortable on the ball and was able to hold possession effortlessly. He also had tremendous vision and a keenly intelligent approach to the game. If he was not receiving passes that were allowing him to score, he could be counted on to win possession further out the field and to create opportunities for other players close to goal with pinpoint passing and creative play. Kieran McKeever, the Derry player who had marked him more often than anyone else in inter-county football, said of him, 'If he gets [the ball] into his hands, there's not much you can do. He's fast on the turn and can wrong-foot anyone. He's a genius. The best forward in Ireland.' In saying this, McKeever perhaps understated the claims of Kerry's Maurice Fitzgerald to that title, but there was no doubt that Canavan and Fitzgerald were in a different league when compared with other forwards in the game.

While all the season's hype had been focused on Jason Sherlock, 1995 was the year of Peter Canavan. And yet, it could easily have been over for him in late June. At half-time in their match against Derry, Tyrone had been three points and two men down. Derry had arrived out for the second half, content in the knowledge that, as favourites for the All-Ireland, with a three-point lead and a two-man advantage, the game was as good as won. Then Tyrone had mugged them. Tyrone had kept possession well and swarmed over Derry's bigger players with speed and determination and had won by a single point. Commentators had fallen over themselves in the rush to the dictionary to find new adjectives to describe Tyrone's second-half performance. Sensational. Awesome. Magnificent. But of the eleven points Tyrone scored that day, Canavan had scored eight.

Having written their name in lights with the victory over Derry, Tyrone went on to suggest that this may have been little more than an out-of-character, mad moment of brilliance by turning in a cumbersome display in overcoming a very ordinary Cavan team in the Ulster final. Early on, Cavan had cut easily through the Tyrone defence and, as the game progressed, Tyrone continually failed to draw more than a goal ahead of a hard-working but limited Cavan side until eight minutes from the end. While some of the team spoke afterwards about their determination to continue Ulster's success at All-Ireland finals, the bookies were lengthening the odds on Tyrone winning the title.

Tyrone had been once more unimpressive in their victory over a spirited Galway side in the semi-final the week before Dublin had played Cork. Although Canavan had scored only 0–5 of his side's 2–13 against Cavan in the Ulster final, it was business as usual in the semi-final with their essential forward scoring 1–7 of Tyrone's 1–13. His contribution that day was even more impressive than his scoring tally made it seem. His goal had kept Tyrone in the game when they appeared to be fading out of contention. When Galway nudged back ahead in the second half, Canavan had hit three points in a seven-minute spell which, once more, turned the match in Tyrone's favour. Canavan had claimed after the Cavan game that his teammates had shown that he was not the only player on display, but all other available evidence seemed to suggest the contrary. The suspicion remained that Tyrone were an ordinary side that had fortuitously found that big guns in Ulster like Down and Donegal had been taken out by others, while Derry had fallen victim to their own complacency. After that, they had tottered through the easier side of the draw into the All-Ireland final. That was not, we were told, the profile of All-Ireland winners. At the same time, Tyrone had beaten everyone who had been put in front of them so far and only had one more game left to win. While Dublin were preparing under the pressing glare of the national (Dublin-based) media, Tyrone were able to prepare in comparative peace and quiet. While Dublin carried the weight of the nation's expectation and of every loss since 1991, no one expected victory of Tyrone except themselves. That was what made them dangerous.

* * *

It was Saturday, a week before the final, that things started to go awry for Dublin. The Dublin squad was playing a practice match with the 'A' team lined out against the 'B' team. Ciaran Walsh's performance in the Cork game had played him into contention for a starting place and he was playing in the full-back line of the A team, alongside Dermot Deasy and Paddy Moran, while Keith Galvin had been moved to the B side. Twenty minutes into the practice match, Dermot Deasy was withdrawn from the game, suffering a disc injury in his back. Intensive treatment was administered, including an epidural injection, to try to ease the problem but to no avail. On Tuesday night the team was announced, with Keith Galvin taking Deasy's place in the full-back line. With a week to go to the All-Ireland final, the man Dublin were counting on to attempt to marshal Canavan was out of the game.

On Wednesday, things got much worse. That evening, Charlie Redmond was out at his local club practising free-kicks. Towards the end of his routine, he placed the ball on the ground for a simple 14-metre free-kick and went through his familiar routine of stepping back, looking at the post, licking his hand and wiping it across his chest, then starting his looping run towards the ball, but as his foot made contact with the ball, he felt a painful twinge high in his thigh. He had torn a muscle. With four days to go to the biggest – and possibly the last – game of his inter-county career, he was in serious trouble. Charlie still carried the burden of the previous year's loss, and his first thoughts were that he would be letting his teammates down again. He went straight to the clubhouse, put ice on his thigh and called Pat O'Neill.

Pat tried to reassure him everything would be all right but they both knew that the problem was potentially serious. Charlie had scored 30 of Dublin's 71 points during the summer so far. Without him Dublin had no consistent and reliable free-taker. This would mean that Dublin might struggle to get scores, but would also mean that Tyrone would feel free to foul Dublin players in possession, knowing that Dublin were less likely to score from the resulting free. Losing Deasy was a blow, but losing Charlie was a potential catastrophe. Injuries had cost Dublin badly in previous years and so the team and management had agreed that no one would start a game unless they were fit to play. The shit was well and truly hitting the fan.

A torn muscle needed time to rest in order to heal, but time was a luxury that was not available. The first task was to keep the injury quiet as much as possible. News of an injury to Charlie would create a media feeding frenzy, could affect the concentration of the rest of the team and, crucially, could make Charlie a target for physical mistreatment on the pitch as had happened to Niall Cahalane two years previously. Luckily there was little time for news to leak out. The team would train only on Thursday and Saturday and excuses could be made that would hide the extent of the problem. Charlie sat out most of Thursday evening's training, but the media were assured that he simply had a bit of a cold, that there was no major problem and that there was no concern about his availability. The rest of the players were so focused on looking after their own section of the field that the sight of Charlie sitting out training did not unduly worry them. On Saturday morning Charlie's injury merited only a paragraph in the newspapers, indicating that there was no doubt that he would play.

But at training on Saturday morning, the alert code switched from amber to red. In order to check how his injury was healing, Charlie lined up a couple of free-kicks but, as he struck them, everyone around the ground became aware of the extent of the problem. After a couple of kicks, the management called Charlie back off the pitch and told him to rest. Pat O'Neill reassured Charlie that he could give him a painkilling injection before the game which would allow him to play, but the worries persisted. Paul Clarke began to practise taking frees. The rest of the players were now aware of the problem but, caught in the anticipation of their own private battle and all its elements, largely did not discuss Charlie's injury with each other. After a short meeting they all headed off to use up the one more day before the final.

Ciaran Walsh headed back to work that afternoon to pass the time and keep his mind off the game. People dropped in to the shop in a steady stream to wish him well and in the blink of an eye, four hours passed. That night he and his wife went out for a pasta meal, he drank a pint of beer and then headed home to watch television. Then he went to bed and slept soundly. Only a few kilometres away from Ciaran Walsh's house, Paddy Russell had booked into a hotel in the west of Dublin in order to avoid having to travel up from Tipperary on the morning of the game. Twice during the night the fire alarm went off and he was woken up. Ruefully, he thought to himself that he would have arrived at the game more rested and refreshed had he taken the train from Tipperary on the morning of the game.

The morning of the match dawned and the sun returned, putting in one last appearance to remind us of our summer, before slipping away to the recesses of winter. I still had no ticket. The night before, as Ciaran Walsh had been out to dinner and Paddy Russell had been en route to Dublin, I had spent the evening touring GAA pubs in Dublin in the hope of picking up a ticket, but there was none to be had. The four years of hype surrounding this Dublin team was coming to a crescendo and everyone in the city wanted to be at the final. The fact that Dublin were roaring favourites only added to the hype, as everyone wanted to be able to tell in future years that they were there the day Dublin won the 1995 All-Ireland. Tyrone people had also travelled in large numbers to the game. Tyrone had reached only the second All-Ireland final in their history and people were worried that they might not live to see them reach a third. As a result, the county had emptied as men, women and children in white and red poured across the border and descended upon Dublin in their droves, all in search of match tickets. On other days the issue for me was about getting a Hill 16 ticket, but not today. Today, just getting inside the famous old ground would be a gargantuan task in itself.

Late the evening before the game, I had come to the realisation that I was going to have to deal with a tout in order to get my ticket. Football fans hate having anything to do with touts, or 'scalpers' as they are called in the US. Through lying, cheating, stealing and the sale of their grandparents into slavery, touts got between our tickets and us and then fed like leeches off our craving. Like drug dealers or solicitors, they made their money out of our misery. We hated them for it but in desperate times men do desperate things. Ticketless and without any word of a ticket to be had, I was going to a tout.

There is a geography of desire and angst that ultimately determines the price which one will pay to a tout for a ticket. Those who will buy well before the game are the most frantic or the most inexperienced and therefore are those who will pay the most for their ticket. Midweek before the game many people are still holding onto tickets for people who may or may not show up on the day and, consequently, it always looked like there were no tickets available at that stage. Time is at this stage on the tout's side. If he doesn't like what you are offering then he can afford to wait, let the days, hours and minutes tick past and let you fester in your own desperation as the throw-in time approaches. Early on match day, touts will be found in the city centre where they might snag some rugby-supporting type for whom the All-Ireland final will be the only Gaelic football match he will see in a decade but who has the money to pay handsomely for the privilege. Those who buy this far out are buying from the first or second tout they see and have no real idea what the actual market value of a ticket is. Like the midweek buyer, they are cash cows, there to be milked. Only as the game approaches and the cash cows dry up do touts start to gravitate towards the stadium and the harder core of supporters.

Those who have the nerve for it prefer to wait close to throw-in before buying from a tout. As throw-in ticks ever closer, suddenly time becomes the friend of the buyer. A match ticket that was worth a small fortune a few hours before becomes worthless once the match has started and so, in the last few minutes before the game, ticket prices tumble on the streets. Yet this waiting strategy has its dangers. With much of Dublin and everyone in Tyrone scavenging for tickets, there was a strong possibility that the tout would have sold his lot and would be relaxing in the pub with a wad of cash in his pocket by the time the game approached. The trick was to ask around, build up a realistic picture of the market value, hang on for as long as you dare and then leap in and haggle.

I made my way into town that morning with 100 pounds in my pocket (my take-home pay at the time was 125 pounds for a half-time job) and with my ears ringing with radio stories of counterfeit tickets. One story said the counterfeits all had the same serial number, while another said that the date was printed in the wrong colour ink. Basically, everyone was saying that there were counterfeit tickets but no one really knew what they looked like. Part of the problem was that I wasn't even sure what a real ticket looked like. I met one person at the bus stop that told me he had got himself a ticket and I asked for a look at it in order to know what a genuine ticket looked like. He looked back at me – a heavy, bald and gruff-talking young man with a nervous look about me – and declined to produce the ticket for inspection. To be fair, I could understand where he was coming from.

On O'Connell Bridge I came across someone selling the *XPress* All-Ireland Special. It bore a picture of Jayo on the front page under a banner headline proclaiming 'It's the Dubs!' The *XPress* had become less visible over the few weeks in the run-up to the All-Ireland and I was glad of the opportunity to get what I hoped would be a memorable keepsake. Then I headed up O'Connell Street, where I met the first of the touts. They were standing halfway up, calling, 'Tickets . . . any tickets . . . buying or selling.' I approached one of them nervously, slowing as I approached him and feeling like I was trying to buy uranium from a rogue Russian agent. 'How much?' I asked furtively. 'Two hundred and fifty quid,' he replied. The ticket he was selling had a face value of nine pounds. I just kept walking, but he called after me, 'You're not going to do any better, pal. I'll see you later.' I hoped he was wrong. I asked the next if he had a Hill ticket. He just laughed. 'There are no Hill tickets. No one has them.' He offered me a stand ticket for 60 pounds, three times its face value but so cheap that I was immediately suspicious. Again, I walked on.

'There are no Hill tickets.' I heard it again and again as I got closer to the stadium. Ticket prices levelled out at just over 100 pounds for a ticket that should have cost nine pounds and showed no signs of dropping further as the match time approached. I watched with growing anxiety as people approached the touts and money changed hands. Each purchase pushed me further and further from getting inside. I was now within earshot of the stadium and could hear the roar of the crowd watching the underage match every time someone scored. Each roar was like an injection of adrenalin pumped into my system, winding me up tighter and tighter until I could take it no longer. Twenty-five minutes before throw-in, and probably just as prices were about to start dropping, I succumbed. With the words, 'There are no Hill tickets' banging around inside my head, I bought a Canal End ticket for 90 pounds and, with ten pounds left to get me though the day and all the way to next Thursday's pay packet, I joined the giddy throng heading down the North Circular Road towards Croke Park.

As always, the crowd flowed like a river down Jones' Road and over the bridge at the Canal. It was here, for the first time, that I became aware just how many Tyrone people had travelled for the game: for the first time all season, the Dubs were genuinely outnumbered by the multitude in red and white. I was going to be among the Tyrone crowd on the Canal End, but, while I would have loved to have been on the Hill, I knew that being in Croke Park would have to be enough. Of course, being on the Hill would have been something special, but it seemed it was not to be. The crowd was packed tightly together as I came over the bridge and began to make my way down the slipway to the Canal End stiles. Suddenly there was a middle-aged, balding Tyrone fan standing in front of me, blocking my way.

'Do you want a Hill ticket?' he asked, a look of intensity etched on his face.

'Of course,' I replied, a little annoyed. This was not the time for stupid rhetorical questions. I started to brush past him.

'No,' he barked. 'Do you want a Hill ticket instead of a Canal ticket?'

'Yes!' I said, somewhat exasperated. Why did he persist in bothering me with these nonsensical questions? There were no Hill tickets. The Canal would have to do.

'Look,' he said, speaking slowly now and articulating every syllable in the hope that I might understand. He drew from his inside pocket a ticket. 'I have a Hill ticket. I want a Canal ticket. Will you swap me for a Hill ticket?' It was like a dam burst and realisation flooded in. I was caught between being embarrassed at my own stupidity and being dumbfounded by the realisation that, against the odds, my Hill ticket had found me.

I leapt forward and hugged him. I could feel he was embarrassed, but I didn't care. The crowd passed around us, no doubt with some wondering briefly what was going on as two heavy, bald men, one in Tyrone colours and one in a Dublin jersey and a cowboy hat, hugged each other. We swapped tickets and shook hands. Then he vanished back into the crowd and I pushed my way against the human tide back up the slipway to the road, and half walked, half skipped my way along the road to join the rest of the lads in our place on the Hill.

* * *

The Dublin team were in the dressing-room by then. Charlie, who had driven in with Mick Deegan, was sitting by himself. He typically headed to the toilets to throw up before a game and now was sitting, eyes closed as if sleeping. The others had made their way to Croke Park in twos and threes. Some had sat watching the underage game for a while, checking how the ball was bouncing and how the pitch was running. Others had headed straight for the dressing-room. Dessie bounced a ball off the wall in the toilets, practising hand passes and foot passes, Paul Curran did some push-ups, while others laughed and joked before finally going quiet and preparing themselves for the match that awaited them. No one was screaming or shouting, no one was leaving their aggression behind them in the changing-room. They had been here before and knew what it was about. Four years had led them to this point; there would be no going back and no countenancing failure. For Ciaran Walsh, it was to be his first senior All-Ireland final. Injury had kept him out the previous year and had caused him to lose his place in the team at the beginning of this season. Now he was sitting in the dressing-room and was about to mark Peter Canavan, the most feared forward in the game. In his mind, he was chewing at the door, anxious to get out on the field and be playing. He was ready.

John O'Leary, as captain, said his final words. He pointed to electrical sockets high on the wall of the dressing-room. For 15 years he had been changing in the same dressing-room but had only ever seen those sockets used once. They had been used for the television lights on the day that Dublin had last won the All-Ireland, 12 years previously. The reason they had never been used since was that no one wants to look at the losers. Pointing at the lights, he told his teammates: 'Make sure they are used today.' The dressing-room door opened and the team took to the field to the sound of the crowd's roar. 'I'll never forget the cauldron, the noise on the pitch that day,' Willie O'Mahony, who was linesman that day, later told me. 'It's different on the pitch, it's a complete din of noise, a great atmosphere.'

Still nobody knew if Charlie would play. Minutes before the game, Charlie had asked for the painkilling injection that Pat O'Neill had promised him the day before. There has been a change of plan, O'Neill told him. After discussion with his medical colleagues they had decided against an injection. 'There are no injections being given. You are either fit to play, or you are not,' O'Neill informed him. Charlie later reflected, 'He had no intention of ever giving me an injection. He was just letting me think that he would.' Maybe they suspected that part of the problem was in Charlie's head. The injury did not seem sufficient to stop him playing, but it had spooked him. He was able to run fine, but he seemed unable to follow through on his kicks. Charlie had been feeling low in himself ever since the injury on Wednesday. They had nurtured him to this point in the hope that once he got out to play, things would come right. But as the team photo was taken, Charlie still had his tracksuit top on while the rest were wearing their jerseys. Much of the crowd was distracted by a crazy fool who had climbed onto the top of the Nally Stand and was sunbathing on the roof near the flagpole just above Hill 16. So distracting was he that many did not see Charlie line up a short free and kick it so limply that it got nowhere near lifting off the ground. But enough people saw it to ensure a massive intake of breath around the ground. People turned to the person next to them and asked what had happened. News of the actual or suspected state of Charlie's leg roared around the ground in a firestorm of agitated conversation. Up on the Hill, all the comfort that had been gleaned from the reassuring leaks to the newspapers vanished. If Charlie was in trouble, then so were we. At the back of the Hill, I felt my stomach lurch. The lads grabbed each other by the shoulders and held on. All eyes were on Charlie as he went to the sideline and conversed with the management. He later recalled, 'I put the ball on the 14-metre line and kicked it straight into O'Leary's hands. It never got off the ground. But I knew I had to just put the pain out of my head. I went onto the field with the intention of not letting it hold me back. I decided that if the thigh was going to go on me it was going to rip from crotch to knee because I was going to go so hard.' For a few moments, 66,000 pairs of eyes were fixed on that huddled conversation, then Charlie took his tracksuit top off while one of the management team ran to let Paddy Russell know the starting team and the list of substitutes, and Charlie took his place for the pre-match parade. In relief and release the crowd began to roar.

It was Charlie who spoke the last words to the team in the huddle on the pitch. 'This is our destiny,' he told them. 'Everything has been leading up to this. The four in a row with Meath, losing to Donegal, Derry, Down . . . It's all behind us and it's all come down to this one day. When you get out of this huddle and go to your man and look him eye to eye you have to say to yourself, "Is it him or me today?" It's up to every man to answer that question.'

In the parade before the match Tyrone refused to march down in front of the Hill, showing us once more that we were feared. Then, as the players took their positions, the crowd began to roar once more, trying to release some of the pent-up nervous energy. Four months – four years – and it all came down to this: seventy minutes of play. Paddy Russell threw in the ball. The game was on.

It was Tyrone that started better. Dublin had become rusty in the four weeks since the Cork game and struggled to match their opponents' pace and intensity early on. Their game plan was immediately evident: get the ball to Canavan. Two minutes into the game, Canavan got away from Walsh and was fouled by Paddy Moran who had come across to cover him. Kicking into the Hill 16 goal and kicking from the hands rather than off the ground, Canavan slotted the free over the bar to put Tyrone one up. A minute later he repeated the feat, kicking off the ground this time, and Tyrone were two ahead. Two minutes later again, Canavan won the ball and played it off to his teammate Jody Gormley who put it over the bar. Tyrone were now three points up, but, with seventy minutes to go in the match including stoppage time, no Tyrone player other than Canavan would score again, and Dublin had not yet started playing.

Dublin needed something to inspire them, something to lift their spirits and their heads. When it came, it came from Keith Barr. Tyrone were trying to prevent the Dublin half-forward line from getting into the game by fouling players out in midfield in the hope that free-kicks from far out would not be scored. With seven minutes gone a free-kick was awarded to Dublin from sixty-five metres out. It seemed an impossible distance, but Keith Barr stepped up to take it. His approach lacked any of the method or precision of Charlie. He gave himself a ten-metre run-up to the ball and then booted it with a tremendous kick that carried it straight and true over the bar. 'I fancied myself to make the point,' he later recalled. 'It was a nice, calm day, the sun was shining. I knew it would either go over the bar or it would go short for someone else. It was a welcome score, it settled us down.' The Hill rose in acclamation of Barr, the heart and soul of the team.

Around the ground, Dublin players started to raise their heads from their own private battles and started to see their teammates. Almost immediately, Dublin players began winning more ball and possession. Two more free-kicks followed in quick succession. The first was taken by Charlie from 15 metres out. Normally it would have been an assured point, but now it took on massive significance. If he couldn't land this one, then there was no point in him being on the pitch. But when Charlie hit it, it sailed over the bar. Paul Clarke followed it a minute later with another free, this time from about 50 metres out. Within four minutes of their first score, Dublin had drawn level. Doubts about Charlie's ability to play had abated and, once he had crossed the white line, he began to play well. It seemed that his movement was relatively unencumbered by his injury.

In the weeks before the final, many had expected an open and flowing game of football. Fifteen minutes in, it was clear that that was not going to be the case. Tyrone were seeking to limit the effectiveness of Dublin's forwards by persistently fouling Dublin's half-forwards. Dublin were responding in kind. Both teams had swamped the middle of the pitch with players in the hope of picking up loose ball, and midfield had developed into a claustrophobic arena of dragging, pulling and fouling, ensuring that Paddy Russell as referee was constantly involved in play. Both teams had conspired to make this a guerrilla war of many clashes. It was not pretty, but its intensity was, in its own way, compelling.

Tyrone were winning more ball than Dublin in the middle of the park but using it poorly. Many of the balls coming in towards Canavan were of poor quality, and Ciaran Walsh was quickly coming to terms with marking the most dangerous forward on the pitch. Balls that did not go to Canavan went to Ciaran McBride, who was winning them but failing to use them. On the other hand, the Dublin forwards were doing more with less. Sherlock was everywhere. He buzzed about, creating spaces for other forwards with distracting runs and winning ball when it came his way. Farrell was at his strong and ruthless best, winning ball with tenacity and taking points with cool precision. In the half-back line, Paul Curran was dominating proceedings, winning ball after ball and carrying or passing it forward to set up attacks. Over the next 15 minutes the game swung back and forth, with Farrell's three scores matched by two frees by Canavan. With 25 minutes gone, Dublin were a single point ahead and the game hung in the balance. The intensity on the pitch had communicated itself to the spectators, who seemed unable to lift their voices and a strange silence hung over the ground. Then came the moment that in any other year would have been the defining moment of the game.

Sherlock had almost got in for a goal a few minutes earlier. Paul Clarke had snapped up a loose ball in the middle of the pitch and had dropped it in towards the goalmouth. It had come to Charlie, who had found Sherlock at an acute angle. His shot had flashed narrowly wide, but it showed nonetheless that Dublin carried the threat of a goal. The next time it was Curran who was the launching pad. He won a ball in the half-back line and found Paul Bealin, who launched it up along the touchline towards Charlie Redmond's position. Neither Charlie nor his marker, Paul Devlin, managed to win the ball and it bounced loose into the space between Jason Sherlock and the man-mountain in the Tyrone goal, Finbar McConnell. The Tyrone centre half-back spotted the danger and left Dessie Farrell to try to reach the ball before Sherlock. Jayo set off like a lithe greyhound while at the same time Finbar McConnell left his goal line and set off like a Sherman tank. For a moment, the ball sat between the three of them as they ploughed towards each other. Sherlock, the smallest man on the field, was racing towards a collision with the two biggest men on the Tyrone team. The difference between Sherlock and McConnell was some 18 cm (7 in.) in height and 32 kg (70 lb) in weight, but Sherlock never flinched.

The ball was 13 metres out from goal when Sherlock reached it, a fraction of a second before the centre half-back crashed into him. As McConnell blotted out the daylight, Sherlock deftly poked the ball goalwards under the advancing goalkeeper and was immediately flattened by the two Tyrone men.

Sherlock's race was over, but the outcome had not yet been decided and now it was Charlie that had to drive himself forward through the pain. With Paul Devlin dragging him back, Charlie hauled himself and his marker forward, resolve and pain etched on his face, determined to reach the ball. If he hadn't got there, the unmarked Dessie Farrell would certainly have finished it, but strikers are required to be selfish and Charlie was going for this one. Collapsing as he reached it, he stuck out his leg and flashed the ball into the back of the empty net. At the far end of the pitch, the Hill erupted. In a match that had tottered back and forth between the combatants, Dublin were four points clear and Charlie Redmond, who had so often carried the weight of Dublin defeats on his own back, had got the touch that finished the goal.

If Charlie's leg was hurting before the goal, it was worse now. The effort of dragging his marker towards goal and of striking the ball while falling had torn his thigh muscle still further. As the green flag waved to signal a goal, he gingerly picked himself to his feet and, a grimace etched across his face, limped heavily away. Getting to half-time without being substituted was now a key concern. As always, the central question after scoring a goal was which side would score next. For five minutes, both teams tore into each other with ferocious determination, but neither could get loose of the other's grasp. Then, suddenly, Paul Curran broke free into space and took on the responsibility himself, dropping the ball over the bar. In the last minute of the half, Dublin and Tyrone once more swapped points. At half-time Dublin were five points clear.

From here, Dublin should have been counting on closing out

the game in the second half. Even with Charlie's injury, other Dublin forwards were taking responsibility on themselves. Paul Clarke, Dessie Farrell and Jim Gavin had all scored. Jason was sniffing at goal chances, had created one and was not far off another. The defence was holding well, Paul Curran was magnificent and the Tyrone attack had, by and large, been reduced to seeking to win frees. From here on out, all other things being equal, Dublin had the maturity, the experience and the ability to close out this game as they had done so many others. But the gods that watch over sport are nothing if not perverse. The one question that had been asked of this Dublin team was whether or not they had the cast-iron will to win. No one doubted their maturity, their experience or their ability. But people did wonder if they found themselves stumbling through the claustrophobic closing moments of an All-Ireland final with victory slipping from their grasp, would they have the will to hang on or would they panic, succumb to despair and let it slip away once more. Far from the second half becoming a holding operation, the Fates that govern sport were determined that it would become a crucible in which the mettle of the Dublin team would finally be tested once and for all.

It was ten minutes into the second half that Pandora's box was opened and the Fates were set free to sting the Dublin team and its followers. Canavan had reeled off three free-kicks to drag Tyrone back into the game and to give them hope once more. Farrell had replied with a well-taken, hard-fought point in front of the Hill to put Dublin three up again. Then a ball was won, inevitably by Paul Curran, and he played it up along the sideline towards Sherlock and Redmond. Sherlock got there first, but as he reached the ball he was flattened by his marker. Paddy Russell blew the whistle to signal a free-kick to Dublin as the ball bounced loose towards Charlie Redmond. Then Redmond too was flattened while trying to pick up the ball. As Redmond lay face down on the ground, a Tyrone player, who had been uninvolved in this passage of play, jogged three or four metres to where Charlie was lying and dropped his knee onto the back of the prone and defenceless player.

Charlie leapt to his feet and, filled with a need for outraged retribution, charged towards the Tyrone man. The linesman, Willie O'Mahony, intervened to separate the two as Charlie's head lurched forward in a headbutting motion. Although no contact had been made with his opponent, Paddy Russell, who was standing only metres away and had a clear view of the incident, had no doubt. Charlie Redmond had intended to strike another player. It was a sending-off offence.

If Russell was clear, however, few others were. The incident had happened along the sideline near the Dublin bench, and Pat O'Neill came charging out to remonstrate with the referee. The Dublin crowd had not only seen the first incident that had given rise to the initial free-kick but had also seen the second when Redmond had been struck when he was face down on the turf. If anyone was to be sent off, we expected it would be a Tyrone player. Some Tyrone supporters in the New Stand beside the incident were half-heartedly gesturing for Charlie to be sent off – something few expected because, given the amount of physical contact in the game, it seemed unlikely someone would be sent off for attempting and failing to actually make contact. But Paddy Russell was adamant. He believed Charlie had attempted to strike a Tyrone player and was to be sent off. At the time, Gaelic games did not use red or yellow cards to signal a warning or a sending-off. The referee simply gestured to the sideline. Already standing at the sideline, Russell held his hand out, formally pointing Redmond off the pitch.

But the confusion was far from over. Indeed, in the days, weeks and years that followed, confusion became heaped upon confusion, in part because Charlie was free to talk about the incident and in part because Paddy Russell, as referee, was forbidden to discuss it. Ten years after the event, a series of newspaper articles would be produced describing the event, all of them suffering some of the same inaccuracies because they lacked both the referee's and the linesman's perspective. It became accepted that Charlie prevailed upon the referee to consult his linesman, who in turn supported Redmond's version of events, that Russell suggested to Charlie that he could play on, and then, two minutes later, on the advice of the same linesman, sent Charlie off a second and definitive time. Immediately after the game, Charlie told an interviewer, 'He sent me off and then changed his mind and told me to stay on and then he re-changed his mind two minutes later and put me off . . . I reacted. The referee says I headbutted him. Now if I headbutted him he'd have a little bit of a cut somewhere on him. I thought it was a terrible decision . . . The linesman told me I was OK . . . It was their ineptitude.' Tyrone, perhaps because they knew that their player had sparked the incident with a foul far worse than Charlie's half-hearted headbutt, didn't challenge this account of events and, as the GAA rules precluded the officials from commenting, Charlie's account became accepted as definitive. Of the 66,000 people in Croke Park that day only the match officials – the referee and his linesmen – actually had to stay impartial. Every other person's perspective was coloured with passion, guilt, anger or grief. This was all the more true in the case of the Dubs who believed every culchie referee was out to get them. In such circumstances few were prepared to even stop to think whether or not Paddy Russell might have had a point.

Ten years later, Paddy Russell still remembered clearly the events of that day. 'Striking or attempting to strike with the head is a sending-off offence. Charlie did throw the head at him. He did. I have no qualms about it. I would do the same thing in the morning. Then I went to Willie O'Mahony, who was the linesman, to ask him who was the Tyrone player involved, because I was going to book him, and he said to me, "I don't know, I didn't get his number" . . . Charlie reckons that Willie O'Mahony told me that I'd got the wrong man and "I'd done nothing" and all this type of thing. Willie O'Mahony didn't say that.' Willie O'Mahony's memory of the incident is the same as Paddy Russell's. 'As far as I know a Tyrone player stamped on his back, and of course Charlie got up and lunged at him. I caught hold of Redmond. Then Paddy ran over and said to me "Was I seeing things, or did he use the head?" I said "He did." That was enough for Paddy. Paddy asked me who else was involved but I didn't catch the number of the Tyrone player. He would probably have got the line as well if I had got his number, but you know the way it is, I had got distracted with holding Charlie back. He was incensed and there was no doubt the Tyrone player did stamp on him. Charlie said afterwards on the radio that the linesman said he was all right, but that never happened.'

Many people when they suffer a shock or a loss go through a kind of grieving process, the first stage of which is denial. It may have been that Charlie was in a state of denial at this stage, unable to accept that he had been sent off in an All-Ireland final and carrying the weight of the possibility that if Dublin lost he would once more blame himself. In this context, he grasped at straws, hoping against hope that he could turn back time and make everything OK again. The conversation between the linesman and the referee perhaps offered him a magical opportunity to make the world right once more. Charlie approached the talking referee and linesman and Paddy Russell gestured him away. Charlie later told me, 'The referee sent me off and I was thinking, "I can't be sent off", and I heard the linesman saying, "No, no, no." So I thought I was OK. I didn't run away or hide. I stood right there when the ball was being thrown up to restart the game. I thought he knew I was still there.'

Russell was now faced with a situation where he and the

linesman were surrounded by arguing players and backroom staff. Given the speed at which players had converged on the incident, it seemed unlikely that any of the other officials had had an opportunity to identify who the guilty Tyrone player was before he was swallowed up in the scrum of bodies. Rather than hold play up unnecessarily in an increasingly tense situation while trying to identify the guilty party, Russell opted to play on and threw in the ball to restart the game. He believed that Charlie had left the field of play. Redmond on the other hand thought he had been reprieved while standing in the shadow of the gallows. Play continued but Dublin now had one player on the pitch who had in fact been sent off. The All-Ireland final was now being played in a twilight zone that was not catered for in any rule book, because such an event was unprecedented.

'I threw in the ball out near the sideline,' Paddy Russell remembered a decade later. 'As far as I was concerned Charlie Redmond had been sent off. The ball broke down toward the Canal End, then it came back up the field and as I'm on my way back up I see Charlie Redmond still on the field! Next thing the ball landed out near the Hogan Stand and the Nally Stand and I ended up giving a free out to Tyrone. I stopped play and I ran over to Willie O'Mahony. Willie was looking out onto the field and I was looking over towards him. I said to him, "Did Charlie Redmond go off?" He said to me, "He did, yeah." I said, "Is the Dublin number 13 still on the field?" He looked out and he said, "Jesus, Paddy! He is." So, I went straight over to Charlie Redmond. I said, "Charlie, you're off." He said "Jesus, Paddy, please don't send me off, it's my last game." I said, "Charlie, I can't do anything about it. You are off." They are the only words that were spoken to Charlie Redmond, and that is exactly what happened.'

Up on the Hill, we were outraged and confused. Like everyone else, we had assumed that Charlie had not been sent off the first time largely because he had stayed on the field and play had continued. Most people assumed that there had been another incident that had caused Charlie to be sent off after play had resumed once more. If there was one, however, we didn't see it. We had spent much of the first half chanting 'The referee's a wanker,' as Russell had awarded free-kicks to Tyrone in front of the Hill. Now, with twenty-five minutes to go in the All-Ireland final, he had sent off Charlie Redmond twice, it seemed, in the space of three minutes. Charlie was more than a hero to the Dublin fans; he was like a mascot. He wore our collective successes and failures on his sleeve like no one else and we loved him for his brashness and his vulnerability. We had never been keen to see Paddy Russell's point of view but now he had become the man who shot Bambi – twice. Whatever else happened, Paddy Russell was not to get his wish of remaining anonymous after the game.

If we were dazed and confused on the terrace, the players on the pitch did not have that luxury. Their half-time lead was draining away, they were just three points up and were missing their star forward with almost half a match to play. If Dublin were to win this All-Ireland, they would have to win it the hard way. It was Keith Barr who now took the lead. He turned to the players around him and told them, 'Lads, we have to work now.' When recalling this incident later, Barr was modest, and focused on those around him: 'I suppose I would have seen myself as an experienced campaigner at the time and I would have brought my experience of the different campaigns to that moment. I felt we were still in this game and that we still had the opportunity to win it. We would often calm one another. And we were very comfortable with each other. Mick Deegan, Paul Curran, Ciaran Walsh were all experienced campaigners, and while it's not nice to have a player sent off in an All-Ireland final, I knew we could deal with the situation.'

No one was blaming Charlie for getting himself sent off; no one was interested in the blame game. The only concern was holding what they had and working twice as hard as the opposition.

And they did. For the next 24 minutes, the game rocked back and forth, and, incredibly, neither team scored. Tyrone made mistakes during this period. Their free player was ineffective and, with the Dublin players increasing their work rate, it seemed at times as if it was Dublin that had the extra man. In the forwards, Sherlock, Mick Galvin and especially Dessie Farrell tore into the opposition, preventing them winning good ball which could be used to set up attacks. The constant movement was exhausting and would eventually take its toll. Dessie Farrell picked up a knock in the side that cracked a couple of ribs, but still he tore into the opposition. The Dublin defence became a study in how to put off attackers without fouling them. They worked hard for each other, ensuring that the player in possession always had an option whether to go short or to go long. This gave them the opportunity to control the pace of the game. As they had done in the Cork match, Dublin slowed the game down, using up time whenever possible but without ever becoming so obvious as to attract the attention of the referee. On occasion, Tyrone players, exasperated by the way the match was playing out, ended up contriving to aid Dublin in this respect by knocking the ball away from free-kicks or kick-outs and allowing Dublin players more time to reset the kick once more. On the sideline, the Dublin management made brave decisions. Recognising that one of the Tyrone forward line was spending most of his time around midfield, Dublin withdrew Keith Galvin and sent on an extra midfielder. When Tyrone spotted the move and pushed the forward back into position, Brian Stynes followed him but Tyrone failed to give the forward good ball that would allow him to test Stynes' skill as a defender. On the sideline the Dublin management decided to make a substitution to use up a few extra seconds. From his spot beside Pat O'Neill, Charlie spotted that Dessie Farrell was the furthest Dublin player from the sideline and so suggested that he be the one replaced, and so Dessie made a long and slow trudge towards the dugout.

It was Dublin who had the scoring chances in this period but, in the absence of Charlie to take the free-kicks, Paul Clarke struggled to find his range and Dublin failed to pull ahead. A ball dropped between Sherlock and Finbar McConnell in the Tyrone goal once more, but this time McConnell got to it first, brushing Sherlock off like a Rottweiler dismissing a toy poodle. All around the ground, the match was played in an atmosphere of eerie silence, as the tension and drama on the pitch got to the crowd. They say that the fastest half of a football match is the half you are winning and the slowest is the half you are losing. The minutes stretched into hours as our anxiety made time elastic. Slowly, but inexorably, the time ticked past until there were only three minutes left on the clock. We began to hope once more.

But the Fates were not finished with our emotions just yet. Neither team had scored for 24 minutes but now, as all of the frenetic activity began to take its toll on the Dublin team, the scores came thick and fast. Tyrone scored first, another free-kick, and closed the gap to two points. In Gaelic games, they say the worst possible lead to have in the last few minutes of a game is a two-point lead. If there is just a point between the teams then the losing side will generally be content to take a point and draw the game. With three points between the sides the losing team need a goal to draw level. But with two points the losing side will often feel the need to go for a goal which, if it is scored, will give them the game. On the Hill we began to panic, but on the pitch the Dublin response was swift. Keith Barr won the ball in centre field and charged forward. He played the ball to Paul Clarke and moved forward to take the return pass. But Clarke, ever determined to try for the magical when the mundane was on offer, turned away from him and from 50 metres out wound up for the shot. Aside from his first-half free-kick, Clarke – Merlin – had not been shooting well all day, and on the Hill I held my head in my hands. 'What the fuck are you doing?' I roared. 'Look at fucking Barr!' Merlin was further from the goal than I was but his poor form had made no impact on his confidence. He let fly and the ball sailed over the bar. It was the best score of the day.

But Tyrone were not beaten yet. Two free-kicks in the space of two minutes ensured that, as the game entered injury time, Dublin were only one point up. The tension was unbearable now. My jaw ached as my teeth ground together and the only sound I could emit was a kind of strangled grunting. My body twitched with each movement, each play on the pitch. All around me men were panicking, but on the pitch Dublin players were stretching muscle and sinew to reach each ball, to put an arm, leg or head in the way. Out on the pitch, Ciaran Walsh blocked out the sounds of the panic which hung around the stadium. 'If they are going to score,' he thought to himself, 'make them work for it. Do not give away any stupid frees. All you can do is stay on your feet, keep your hands off them. Push them out. Don't go lunging in on a tackle that you know you are not going to make. Just play clever.' Up on the Hill, shrill voices were howling, 'Blow the whistle, ref. It's over time. Come on, for fuck sake. Blow the whistle, blow it up.'

With seconds left, the ball broke free to the Tyrone captain. He was in space and might have tried to go for a point himself but opted instead to punt the ball into the danger area in front of goal. John O'Leary, ever the man to dominate his square, called for it and Dublin players stood off as O'Leary leapt. But as he took off he realised he wasn't going to make it. He clattered into the back of Paddy Moran and so was off balance and stretching when his fist made contact with the ball. As a result he didn't get sufficient clearance on it and it dropped 20 metres out from goal, right beside the man who had already that day set a record for points scored in an All-Ireland final, Peter Canavan. Unbelievably, Canavan slipped.

As the man with perfect balance and the agility of a cat turned to take the ball, his feet went out from under him. The ball bounced once, twice, losing height each time. Canavan was stretched along the grass, the ball bouncing past him. Ciaran Walsh was bearing down on his position at breakneck speed. Paddy Russell was only two metres further back. As the ball dropped towards the grass once more Canavan reached out and pushed it towards Sean McLaughlin, a Tyrone half-back who was tearing forward in space. McLaughlin collected the ball and booted it over the bar. On the Hill we cursed with venom. Fuck! A draw. A fucking draw. Shit. Piss. Bollocks. Fuuuuucccckkkk! All my tension had turned to anger. On the sideline, Pat O'Neill shook his head and began to ponder the replay. Then, one of the lads beside me grabbed my shoulder. 'Look,' he shouted in my ear, his arm pointing towards the Dublin goalmouth at the Canal End. Then I saw it. Paddy Russell was standing, arm stretched towards the Hill 16 end, indicating a free-kick to Dublin. 'It's not a point. It's disallowed. Canavan must have handled the ball on the ground,' he bellowed in my ear as he grabbed me in a bear-like grip. Incredulity turned to elation. As John O'Leary kicked the ball out, Russell blew the whistle to signal full-time. In the centre of the field, Keith Barr threw his arms to the heavens in a victory salute. Dublin had won by a single point.

In that moment I was alone in a tumult of noise and jumping, shouting bodies. The lads were slapping each other on the back, hugging each other and dancing. I was getting jostled as lads slapped me on the shoulder or pushed against me as they jumped, but it was like I was watching it all on a television with the sound turned low. The deathly silence that had gripped the crowd for what seemed like forever was gone and the Hill began to sing, 'Come on you boys in blue, come on you boys in blue ...' The lads raised their arms and their voices in acclaim of the team – including number 13 sitting on the sideline – but I just stood, trembling, all the energy drained from my body. Then I sighed deeply with a sense of release, looked to the blue sky overhead and, in that moment, I knew everything was right in the world.

* * *

Down on the pitch it was bedlam. Like me, Pat O'Neill had thought that Tyrone had levelled with the last kick of the game. As he heard the final whistle he turned to Fran Ryder and said, 'Back to training on Tuesday, Fran.' Ryder swept him off his feet. 'What are you talking about? We won. We won!' Ryder roared into his ear as the jubilant crowd engulfed them.

'Nothing teaches you or coaches you for that moment,' Dessie Farrell later told me, 'and then it's all over. You are left trying to retrace, relive, remember, recall, to bring it all back. When the final whistle blows, you feel every emotion under the sun. You would love to be able to bottle it before it dissipates, to try to remember it. But it would never be the same. You would never reach the same crescendo again. But that's what drives you on: if you could have it one last time, what would you give? Did I remember it properly, would I do anything different? You would like to freeze time at that stage.'

All around the ground Dublin fans were charging onto the grass, turning it into a sea of blue and navy. The players were swallowed up by the multitude and assaulted with a cascade of jubilant back slaps. Paul Clarke, whose magical point had turned out to be the decisive score, was lost in the crowd of celebrating fans when suddenly his father appeared in the crowd. He looked at his father and saw tears streaming down his face. Suddenly he felt his own tears gush forth and he hugged his father amidst the crowd and the two of them cried. Jayo, who had managed to swap jerseys with a Tyrone player before the tidal wave of supporters struck, was carried aloft towards the Hogan Stand where the Sam Maguire trophy was to be awarded. There, John

O'Leary and his vice-captain, man of the match Paul Curran, ascended the steps to be awarded the trophy. As they lifted the famous old trophy aloft, they began to hear a familiar sing-song chant as the crowd saluted their favourite, all of whose sins were now washed away: 'Char-lie, Char-lie, Char-lie, Char-lie . . .'

After the presentation, the crush of supporters on the pitch meant that the Dublin team could not get back to their dressing-room and so they were brought to a car park at the back of the Hogan Stand to wait while the supporters left the pitch. There, Ciaran Walsh sat down on the side of a fountain beside a fan who was smoking a cigarette and furiously describing the match to someone on a mobile phone. Walsh had borne the arrows of outrageous fortune as much as any player on the Dublin team. He had suffered through the 1991 series against Meath, had been dropped for the 1992 season and had missed out on the 1994 final through injury. As he sat down beside the fan on the fountain, he tapped him on the arm. 'Can I take a cigarette off you?' he asked. The fan looked at him, then, realising who was beside him, abruptly hung up the phone. 'Take the lot,' he said to Walsh, pushing the 20 cigarettes into his hand, before adding, 'Can you sign my programme?' As Walsh began to sign, the fan looked up and, like a kid waking up to discover that Santa had visited, realised that he was surrounded by the entire Dublin team. Walsh tried to return the fan's cigarettes but he wouldn't take them. 'Hold on to them. If I see you later, I'll get them back. If not, enjoy them,' he said. Then, hardly believing his luck, he made his way among the newly crowned All-Ireland champions collecting signatures. As Walsh sat dragging on his cigarette it occurred to him that this was what made sport special. That night the fan would be in a pub telling his mates about how he had found himself surrounded by the Dublin team only minutes after the final whistle. He could almost hear his voice retelling the story to his incredulous mates: 'I'm telling you! Ciaran Walsh even took my ciggies. I swear!' Throughout Dublin and in Irish bars around the world other people would equally be telling and retelling their stories of the day. That was the magic of Gaelic football: everyone had a story to tell.

Eight

Western Bound Blues

THE DUBLIN TEAM THAT had dominated Gaelic football throughout the early 1990s had at last won their All-Ireland and earned the right to be recognised as one of the great teams. As Charlie Redmond later recalled, 'If you look at the years 1991 to 1995, we were only a few scores away from being the greatest team to ever play for Dublin. It was that close. And we played at a time when it was harder to win than in the 1970s because back then there were only two or three competitive teams. We had the Ulster teams, Kildare, Meath, and Cork as well. And we had Mick O'Dwyer and Sean Boylan, probably two of the top five managers in the history of the game. Those were tough years in which to be trying to win an All-Ireland.' Had the ball bounced differently, that Dublin team might have won three or four All-Irelands and could have been remembered in the same reverential tones as the Dublin team of the '70s, but that was not to be. Had Mark O'Connor or Peter Canavan kept their footing at crucial times they might have won none at all. But they will be remembered as a team who suffered hard losses and who found redemption by winning the hard way through a triumph of will.

After the All-Ireland victory Pat O'Neill and his management team did not seek reappointment and a new management team was put in place for the 1996 season. Some of the players that people had expected to retire – like Charlie and John O'Leary – discovered that they still loved football and so played on. Not everyone was afforded that opportunity. The summer of 1995 had been the summer of Jayo, when a young kid buzzed through the world of Gaelic football and rewrote the rule books while scoring goals in his stocking feet. The week after the All-Ireland final, Dublin played in a charity match against a 'Rest of Ireland' selection. Thirteen minutes into the second half, Jayo-mania swept the crowd and the fans invaded the pitch, clamouring for a touch of their hero and causing the match to be abandoned. But the new Dublin manager didn't take to Dublin's young, fast and mobile goalscoring hero, and Jayo was dropped to make way for Joe McNally. Ironically, McNally had been Dublin's 19-year-old star when they had previously won the All-Ireland in 1983. By 1996, however, he was a lumbering heavyweight of a full-forward, still a good footballer but far from light on his feet and hardly a man for the future. The summer had been abuzz with stories of English Premiership soccer teams signing Jayo but that never came to pass. Jayo did play professional soccer in Ireland, became a television presenter – his good looks and boyish charm making him a natural – and also fronted the government's national anti-racism campaign, but it was for his exploits in a Dublin jersey that he was best known. For much of the next decade Jayo would battle on against the Fates and sometimes unappreciative managers, facing prejudice of many types, all the time yearning to play in a Dublin shirt.

Paul Clarke, who had scored the goal against Meath and the decisive point in the All-Ireland final and who had won an All-Star award for his performance throughout the season, also found himself out of favour with the new management. In 1995 he scored the goal that buried Meath in the Leinster final. In 1996 he watched the Leinster final from Hill 16. The new manager identified that, in his view, Dublin had peaked too early in the 1995 season and so he brought in new training methods. Perhaps most crucially, he took a somewhat softer line with experienced players than the rather disciplinarian approach of Pat O'Neill. Sated by their All-Ireland win, some of the players took advantage of this, and their standards began to drop.

It was widely expected that the Meath manager Sean Boylan would resign after Dublin defeated Meath by ten points in the 1995 Leinster final. Meath greats Brian Stafford and Robbie O'Malley were substituted that day and never played for Meath again. It was also the last game in the 20-year career of Colm O'Rourke, who had probably been Meath's best player on the day. Many commentators predicted that the balance between the two teams had been decisively shifted by Dublin's victory and that it would be many years before Dublin would again lose to Meath. Keith Barr was not convinced, however. 'Meath will be back next year, the hype will be just the same and they will be just as hard,' he told reporters after the match. 'They will want to redeem themselves. It's not the end. It just rolls on for everyone.' As it turned out, Boylan did not resign. The following year Boylan's new-look Meath team faced Dublin in the Leinster final. Dublin led by two points with ten minutes to go but, when the inevitable Meath onslaught began, Dublin lacked the determination to answer it. Dublin lost their Leinster title by two points and began the worst losing streak the team had seen in three decades. Meath marched on to claim the 1996 All-Ireland title. Three years later, Boylan's Meath claimed another.

Gradually the great Dublin team of the early 1990s was broken up by retirements. John O'Leary went in 1997, having played in a record 70 consecutive championship games over 18 years. Charlie Redmond, Keith Barr, Ciaran Walsh and Paul Curran all took their bow over subsequent years. In the years after 1995, Meath, Kildare, Laois and Westmeath would all beat Dublin on their way to claiming Leinster titles. Kildare at the time were managed by Mick O'Dwyer, Dublin's nemesis when he was manager of Kerry in the '70s. In 2003 it was Laois's turn. They won the Leinster title, beating Dublin on the way and playing a wonderfully exuberant brand of attacking football. Amongst their players was Ian Fitzgerald, who had got the two scores that had drawn the underage game on the day Dublin beat Laois in Navan. Damien Delaney and Hughie Emerson, survivors from the excellent Laois team of 1995, still featured in the squad. Laois were managed, inevitably, by Mick O'Dwyer. The following year it was Westmeath's turn to beat Dublin on their way to their first ever Leinster title.

Football changed too in the years after 1995. In 1997 and 1998 Kerry and Galway won All-Ireland titles playing an open and fluid style of football which showed just how grim the matches of the 1980s and early 1990s had been. The trend continued and football in general became faster, more flowing and – with the possible exception of Armagh – more joyful. It may be that, in the future, people will look back at this time and call it a golden age of football. If so, it will be one that took place without any significant input from the Dubs.

* * *

Paddy Russell had hoped that his role in the final of 1995 would be a minor one. Like all referees, he knew that if people noticed a referee at a match it was usually to complain about him. The constant fouling of both teams had ensured that he would come to prominence on the day. Sending off Charlie Redmond and the confusion that surrounded the incident ensured that the ire of Dublin fans would be heaped upon his shoulders. Disallowing the levelling point in the last seconds of the game ensured that Tyrone fans would be equally baying for his blood.

Later, the media would examine these incidents with more forensic care than is given to most crime scenes. Endless video replays would be scrutinised in order to see if Canavan had indeed touched the ball while it was on the ground when playing it out to Sean McLaughlin. Many of those in the ground thought that the ball had bounced fractionally off the ground before Canavan touched it, but the ball had clearly been losing height with each bounce and it did appear from some camera angles to be trickling along the ground when Canavan made contact. Television replays proved inconclusive and the inquest rumbled on. Ten years later, Russell was adamant that the ball was on the ground when Canavan touched it. 'I walked off that field like I would walk off any field. I'm not saying I'm perfect or anything like it, but the decisions I made, I have no qualms with them and I still, to this day, think I would make the same decisions again.' Part of the folk belief about the GAA at the time was that referees were encouraged to give rise to draws in order to ensure a replay and the gate receipts from another full house. Had Paddy Russell allowed Tyrone's point at the end it would have meant a draw, a windfall of ticket money to the GAA and accusations that he had played for a draw. Instead, he was accused of favouring Dublin, perhaps because he was trying to even things up for sending off Charlie Redmond. 'I never thought of it like that,' Russell later remembered. 'The thought never entered my mind, and if it did enter into my mind I would say to myself, "Don't ever referee again."' Russell was one of those on the field closest to the incident and had a clear view of it. He was in no doubt that Canavan had handled the ball on the ground. Probably the only person closer to the incident than Russell was Ciaran Walsh. He too is clear: 'I have to say, it was on the ground. It didn't bounce. He was dead right. I was literally two yards away from Canavan and Paddy Russell was about another three away. He was looking directly at it.'

Of the 66,000 people in Croke Park that day, Russell and his officials were the only ones that were impartial. Everyone else had a vested interest. The players on either team would have happily broken the rules, cheated or stolen if it had meant victory. Both sets of fans were only ever going to see the fouls committed by the opposition. Even the media were not strictly impartial because they did not want to just report events – they also wanted to sell newspapers and advertising. Scandal, debate and controversy were always good for selling newspapers, and the media, both television and press, whipped up the controversy after the match. There were some reasonable, measured voices in the press, but they were few. As Paddy Russell walked off the pitch that day, he had no idea he was walking into a whirlwind. That night the television coverage focused intently on both incidents, with pundits delightedly blaming Russell for the way they turned out. The following day, the *Irish Times* carried an extensive interview with Charlie Redmond who had moved through the grieving process from denial to anger and was now busily blaming Russell for everything. His words fed the fire and it burned for days. The day after the match there was no subject on radio talk shows but Paddy Russell. People who knew little about the game or its rules rang radio stations to criticise the referee. 'What would a man from Tipperary know about football?' they said about Russell, who had been playing football for the best part of three decades, refereeing it for 20 years and whose experience at All-Ireland level dated back to 1982.

On the Monday after the All-Ireland there was a dinner for the players and officials in a Dublin hotel. The controversy was raging, and there was even some debate as to whether or not Dublin would be stripped of the title because Charlie Redmond had been playing illegally for part of the match. Russell considered not turning up as the savage media circus was at the time hanging him out to dry. He wanted to avoid meeting people because they would only want to talk about the events of the game. All he really wanted to do was go home. Eventually, however, he decided to go. Photographers followed him around, looking to get a photo in which he looked strained or hunted. Ultimately they got a suitable one and it appeared in the next day's papers. But, as he sat at the meal, things began to turn. Charlie Redmond wandered over to him and had a few conciliatory words. Ciaran Corr, the Tyrone captain, approached him to let him know that the Tyrone players had met and agreed that they had no complaints with him. When he got home his phone was ringing with messages of support. As the national airwaves continued to be filled with strident voices of criticism, the letters of support from total strangers began to arrive at his house. Some were simply addressed to 'Paddy Russell, Referee, Tipperary' but they found him nonetheless.

Many people would have retired from refereeing after that. Russell received nothing out of refereeing except the enjoyment of being involved in Gaelic games. He had already refereed in the national club final, in the league final, in the Munster final, in two All-Ireland finals and in exhibition matches in Scotland, Toronto and England. There was no honour left in the game that he had not already achieved. But he never seriously considered giving it up. His wife, Margaret – herself a knowledgeable football supporter – encouraged him to stay at it as long as he was enjoying it. When the National League began a few weeks later, GAA head office appointed him to one of the major games in the top division. Had they appointed him to a division three or four match, it would have seemed a signal that they doubted his capacity and, under such circumstances, he might have considered resigning. Instead, they reaffirmed their faith in him.

Before the final, Paddy Russell had been asked if he favoured changing the rules in order to introduce more support for the referee. He indicated that some such changes would perhaps make a difficult job a lot easier for the referee but that he would operate the rules however they were. Immediately after the final, some referees began to point out that much of the confusion arose because the referee pointing towards the sideline was an ambiguous signal and that the game needed to learn from other codes by adopting a system of yellow and red cards for warnings and sendings-off, such as were used in soccer. The thought of borrowing something from soccer was distasteful for many who still saw Gaelic games as an antidote to 'English' games, but the case for change was unavoidable. Within a short period such a system was adopted.

Ten years later, Paddy Russell still had the video of the 1995 All-Ireland final but had never watched it. 'It still hurts,' he said. 'All the controversy and fuss.' A few years later, after his story appeared in a book on Gaelic games referees, one of the Dublin squad of 1995 wrote to him to express his regret for how things had transpired. 'He didn't deserve all the abuse he got,' Ciaran Walsh told me ten years after the 1995 final. 'To me, he did as good a job as any referee could have done on the day.' Charlie Redmond too feels that Russell did not deserve the criticism which he received. 'He is a GAA man and he shouldn't be subject to that sort of criticism, in the same way as any player shouldn't.' A few days after the final, Charlie appeared before a disciplinary panel to answer for his sending-off: 'I said that I hope Paddy and I can share a drink sometime and if he got any criticism on account of me I would apologise if it makes the situation better. I was trying to make a gesture. Ultimately the man has to go to work the next day – as we all have to – and he shouldn't have to bear that criticism.'

Charlie still feels, however, that he was wrongly sent off. 'I went at him, and I had my head down to protect myself. I never intended to headbutt him. I ran at him to square up to him. I made a mistake in what I did and I think Paddy made a mistake in what he did. He might not admit to it and he doesn't have to, it's all in the past now. History is history. That's all that counts.'

* * *

Peter Canavan was the player of 1995. He was the year's top scorer and he set a point-scoring record in that year's All-Ireland final, scoring 11 of Tyrone's 12 points and providing the final pass for the twelfth, yet he finished the year without an All-Ireland medal. The following year, Tyrone once more made the All-Ireland semi-finals, where they played a cynical Meath side. Early in the game, two Meath players clattered into Canavan and injured him badly, making him ineffective for the rest of the match. Without his influence, Tyrone were easily beaten. It looked then as if Canavan would be one more great player to never win an All-Ireland.

In 2003, Tyrone reached the All-Ireland final once more. In the semi-final, however, Peter Canavan had fallen in a crumpled heap, having damaged his ankle ligaments. It seemed inconceivable that he would be fit for the final. He wasn't, but he played anyway. In the first half he was an inspiration to the young players around him, giving them the belief that they could wrestle the title from Armagh, the reigning All-Ireland champions. Canavan bowed to the inevitable and was substituted at half-time. Then, with ten minutes to go and with his young teammates under pressure as the final whistle approached he, incredibly, retook the field once more. His return produced a joyous response from Tyrone fans all around the stadium and raised his teammates' spirits once more. There was joy and relief etched on Peter Canavan's face when, as captain, he triumphantly raised the Sam Maguire trophy aloft, but there was something else too. Redemption.

* * *

In September 2005, a decade after the 1995 final, Paddy Russell refereed the All-Ireland semi-final between Tyrone and Armagh. The score was level after one of the finest and most intense games of the year as the clock ticked into the second minute of injury time. Underneath the Hogan Stand, a Tyrone player won the ball and his jersey was tugged as he moved forward. Perhaps some referees would not have given the free-kick, preferring instead to leave it as a draw and ensure a good crowd and healthy gate receipts for a replay, but not Paddy Russell. If he saw a free, he gave a free, irrespective of the context. Just as had happened ten years previously, he gave the free as he saw it. For a moment there was a debate as to which Tyrone player would take the difficult free-kick, then up stepped their second-half substitute, the now 34-year-old Peter Canavan. 'This is it,' Russell said to Canavan as he picked up the ball. It was to be the last kick of the game. With cool assurance, Canavan slotted the ball over the bar and kicked Tyrone into an All-Ireland final. Three weeks later, Canavan scored a crucial goal that helped Tyrone beat Kerry in the final and win their second title in three years. On two occasions, ten years apart, Paddy Russell made what he believed to be the right call. On one occasion it cost Tyrone a second shot at the All-Ireland. On the other, it put them on the road to the title. In a strange way, it seemed like some sort of karmic closure.

* * *

It is perhaps understandable that, despite winning their All-Ireland in 1995, some of the Dublin team of that era still have regrets about that period. More than a decade on, Charlie Redmond still cannot let himself forget the penalty miss that he believes cost Dublin the 1994 All-Ireland: 'I am very hard on myself when I make mistakes. I don't know why I make them and I try to analyse them. Even today, 13 years later, I still blame myself for missing that penalty against Down. I will never be able to forgive myself for that.' Nonetheless, the victory of 1995 allows him to put all that in some context: 'I can look back and I can wonder what it would be like if I hadn't won it. I honestly can't imagine what it would have been like. People tell you it's all about the medals, but my medals were stolen a long time ago. It's not about the medals. It never was about the medals. It's about the memories.'

Keith Barr, unlike Charlie, does not let the past weigh upon his mind. For him the penalty miss in the final match of the 1991 saga against Meath is regrettable, but not something that bothers him. While Charlie used his regret to drive him on, Keith found it a burden best dispensed with. As with Charlie Redmond though, for Keith the medal is not the issue: 'Do I polish my medal?' he asks, once more asking questions for himself to answer, 'I haven't seen it since the day I got it, and that's the God's honest truth. No more than the penalty affected me after 1991, I don't think the All-Ireland affected me. I believe I am the same person. I hope I am.' But for Keith, like Charlie, the memories of the team are what is now important: 'I had a lot of experiences with a great Dublin team, and with great Dublin players. There was a lot of personalities on that team. A lot of fellas were like chalk and cheese, there was great friendships, great hatreds, there was great respect, great arguments, great love affairs. Whatever way you want to look at it, we were a team. We were made up of so many different individuals. And I believe that if we didn't have all of those individuals, we never would have won an All-Ireland. And we had a lot of fun. We had a lot of pain in our journeys, but I believe we had more fun than pain. We had mighty days.'

* * *

In September 1996, almost a year to the day after John O'Leary lifted the Sam Maguire trophy, I left Dublin. I travelled west, to take up a job in Limerick. Friends told me not to worry, that a job would turn up in Dublin and that it would not be long before I was back in the Old Town. For a year I spent my Friday evenings on the train to Dublin and my Monday afternoons making the return trip. After a year of shuttling back and forth across the country I grew tired of travelling and decided to make a go of it in Limerick. I started to stay in Limerick for the weekends. It turned out that the Limerick nightlife wasn't bad and I quickly grew to realise that there were real benefits to living outside Dublin. My rent in Limerick was less than half of what it would have been in Dublin and instead of spending hours sitting in traffic every day I was able to walk home from work in a few minutes. On every subsequent visit to Dublin I found the traffic chaos more and more infuriating. I began to realise that drivers in Dublin were more aggressive than in the rest of the country. I still missed some things in Dublin, like a night out in the Olympia nightclub and getting the Sunday papers on the way home on Saturday night. But, over the next few years, as Dublin's traffic got worse and worse and rents skyrocketed, I realised that Dublin's attractions were less and less a compensation for its costs.

Two weeks before Dublin won the football All-Ireland in 1995, County Clare won the hurling All-Ireland for the first time in nine decades. Later, I ended up living in Clare, in a rural village to the west of the Shannon. Once upon a time this was a typical rural Irish village, with seven pubs, two churches, a grocery and a chip shop. Now it also has a laundrette, a Chinese takeaway and an Indian restaurant, while one of the shops now stocks Polish newspapers and beer. The people who lived on my street there included those born in the US, Africa, the UK and France. Like the rest of Ireland, this village is a cosmopolitan place now, where a diversity of accents can be heard on any street corner. In this respect, as in so many, there is little, if any, difference between city and country now in Ireland; the huge social differences that separated Dublin from the rest of the country in the '70s and '80s are fading rapidly. I loved living in Clare, but being from somewhere matters as much to me now as it did in the summer of 1991, and for that reason, so does football.

Croke Park is different now. The redevelopment means that you can buy a coffee on the Hill these days, and the dirty old toilets that needed to be monitored by the Centre for Disease Control are a thing of the past. So too is the mad crush behind the goal: that space is now marked by two yellow stairwells either side of a low barrier that separates the Hill from the Nally terrace. There is no doubt that the changes have made the Hill a safer and less forbidding place, but something has been lost in the process too. The mad, savage and joyous intensity of that space behind the goal is only now recaptured in fleeting moments.

I still go back to Dublin of course, and, as the summer approaches I can hear my Dublin accent get stronger once more as the championship season comes on. I try to get to all the championship matches still, though it is no longer a case of rolling out of bed and wandering up to Croke Park like it used to be. These days championship matches involve saying goodbye to my wife and my daughter early in the morning as I leave to get to the train station in Limerick and often mean returning home sometime after midnight. I wouldn't miss it for the world, though. As I head off into each summer morning, I still have that ache in the pit of my stomach and I still expect to arrive home hours later, exhausted and hoarse from roaring on the boys in blue.

Acknowledgements

THERE ARE MANY PEOPLE who helped me to write this memoir. They include Jacqueline and Jim Tormey, Noreen Lynch, Florence Macken, Sean de Brúin and Tony Lyons. Ruairi Walsh was an invaluable source for helping me check facts as well as a critical reader and a good friend. My thanks are also due to Carmel Hinchion and to Ollie McGarr for their support, help and encouragement. I know it was not easy for a woman from Cork and a man from Kildare to offer such support to this project. Conversations on Jones' Road and Hill 16 with Pete Keohane and Conor Ryan helped to hone some of my ideas and to stir memories. I am also indebted to Fiona and Anne Looney for their help and support. While it hardly needs saying, whatever errors remain are my responsibility alone.

I am deeply indebted to Ciaran Walsh, Dessie Farrell, Charlie Redmond, Willie O'Mahony, Keith Barr and to Paddy and Margaret Russell for their hospitality and their generosity with their time and their recollections.

I am also indebted to Bill Campbell for taking the chance, and to Graeme Blaikie for bringing the book on.

My deepest debt of gratitude goes to Kitty, for years of support in a thousand ways, to Christine for her love and willingness to listen to endless tales of the Dubs, and to Charlotte, for her companionship while I was writing as well as for her help with the typing.

Notes

Prelude
Ciaran Walsh's view of the 1994 final comes from my interview with Walsh. Charlie Redmond's account of the penalty comes from my interview with him.

Chapter One
The malaise in the Dublin squad in spring 1995 is described in John O'Leary's autobiography, as is O'Leary's injury in 1994. The malaise and recovery of the team was also described in the interview with Walsh. Dessie Farrell, Keith Barr and Charlie Redmond took a different view and felt that the early part of the season was little different from other seasons. The pranks within the Dublin team also come from those interviews and from Dessie Farrell's autobiography. Keith Barr's quote is from my interview with him. Grant Fox's influence on Charlie Redmond and the account of the aftermath of the 1994 penalty miss come from his chapter in Eamonn Rafferty's *Talking Gaelic*. Other information comes from Tom Humphries' *Irish Times* article 'Charlie's on and off day' (18/9/95). Quotations and further details come from my interview with him. Sherlock's basketball credentials and his formative influences, and Danny Culloty's San Francisco childhood come from Tom Humphries' interviews in *Green Fields: Gaelic Sport in Ireland*. Paddy Cullen's infamous 'shoot 'em dead' speech is described in both John O'Leary's and Dessie Farrell's autobiographies. Details on his management style are based on O'Leary's account.

Chapter Two

Many of the detailed memories of Kildare's game with Louth were revived for me by the account of the match in Paul Healy's *The Search for Sam: The All-Ireland Football Championship '95*. Details of Barr's and Walsh's injuries and recuperation come from my interviews with them. The description of the lead into the Louth game comes from my interview with Dessie Farrell. Paddy Russell's childhood memories are from my interview with him. The M. Engel quote from *The Guardian* is quoted on page 140 of Cronin's *Sport and Nationalism in Ireland: Gaelic Games, Soccer and Irish Identity since 1884*. The economic data on the late 1980s comes from page 144 of Richard Breen et al., *Understanding Contemporary Ireland*. Emigration figures come from page 151 of Hillary Tovey and Perry Share's *A Sociology of Ireland,* second edition. The Roddy Doyle quote comes from pages 20–1 of 'Republic is a Beautiful Word – Republic of Ireland, 1990' in Nick Hornby (ed.), *My Favourite Year: A Collection of New Football Writing*.

Chapter Three

Walsh's long wait and his recollections of 1974 are from my interview with Walsh. My memories of Dublin's game against Laois were stirred by the account of the day in Paul Healy's *The Search for Sam: The All-Ireland Football Championship '95*. Paul Clarke as Merlin comes from Tom Humphries' *Irish Times* interview with him, 'Merlin wants the magic to show in every match' (19/8/95). Humphries' comments on the Laois game come from the *Irish Times* article 'Determined Dublin See off Laois Challenge' (10/7/95).

Chapter Four

References to Jack Mahon are from his *A History of Gaelic Football*, pages 190–2 and page 194. Quotes from Colm O'Rourke are from his autobiography, *The Final Whistle*, pages 153–4 and page 160. Much of the description of the Dublin v. Meath rivalry also draws on O'Rourke's book. Barr's memory of the penalty is from my interview with him. The Con Houlihan quote is from page 45 of his book, *More than a Game: Selected Sporting Essays*. The John O'Leary quotes are from pages 79 and 81 of his autobiography, *Back to the Hill*. The G. Gordon Liddy quote is from his book *Will*, pages 156–7.

Chapter Five

The Liam Hayes quote comes from an *Irish Times* article entitled 'Watching from the sideline, they are indeed a funny pair' (29/7/95). Ciaran Walsh's Hill 16 experience is from my interview with him. Some of the quotes attributed to Dessie Farrell in the week before the Meath game are from Tom Humphries' *Irish Times* interview with him, 'Fulcrum for the Frontline' (29/7/95). The rest of the detail is from my interviews with him, Ciaran Walsh and Keith Barr. Paul Clarke on the importance of Hill 16 comes from Tom Humphries' *Irish Times* interview with him, 'Merlin wants the magic to show in every match' (19/8/95). My memories of Dublin's game against Meath were stirred by the account of the day in Paul Healy's *The Search for Sam: The All-Ireland Football Championship '95*. The quote attributed to him comes from page 112 of that book. Quotes from Charlie and Paul Curran after the game are from Tom Humphries' *Irish Times* articles 'Familiarity breeds content and context' and 'Doctor lauds the benefits of new transfusion' (31/7/95). Charlie's account of his best-ever score comes from my interview with him.

Chapter Six

The Louis Walsh quote is from Patsy McGarry's *Irish Times* piece '"Something Special" strikes from the heart of the Dubs' (5/8/95). Con Houlihan's brief autobiography is from his *XPress* article 'The leaving of Castle Island' (29/6/95). Eamonn Sweeney's Con Houlihan story is on page 200 of his book *The Road to Croker: A GAA Fanatic on the Championship Trail*. The account of Tompkins' 1990 injury is based on the account in Colm Keane's book *Gaelic Football's Top 20*, pages 157–8. The Mark/Alison O'Connor story is from pages 237–8 of Burke's *Press Delete: The Decline and Fall of the Irish Press*, while the court's reference to the attitude of the *Press* shareholders is from the same source, page 234. Niall Cahalane's 1993 final experience is from an *Irish Times* interview entitled 'The passion and pragmatism behind the tough customer' (22/7/95). Keith Barr's quotes are from my interview with him. My memories of the match day were rekindled by the account of the day in Paul Healy's *The Search for Sam: The All-Ireland Football Championship '95*. Mark Farr's gesture on Charlie Redmond's behalf is from my interview with Redmond.

Chapter Seven

Comments on Paddy Russell from the week before the final are from Sean Kilfeather's *Irish Times* article 'Central Player Seeks Cameo' (16/9/95). Details on Jackie Carey and Con Martin are from Peter Byrne's book *Football Association of Ireland, 75 Years*. The deaths of Sean Fox, Aidan MacAnespie, Tony Kane, Inan Ul-haq Bashir and John Jeffries are described in David McKittrick et al.'s *Lost Lives*. Seamus Harvey's death is described in Toby Harnden's *'Bandit Country': The IRA and South Armagh*. The McCafferty reference is from Eamonn Rafferty's *Talking Gaelic*. The quotation from Dr Paisley is from page 138 of Susan McKay's *Northern Protestants: An Unsettled People*. The story about Canavan as a schoolboy and the Kieran McKeever quote come from Sean Moran and Tom Humphries' *Irish Times* article 'The wiles of Canavan' (16/9/95). John O'Leary's speech before the final comes from the account in his book *Back to the Hill*. Charlie's pre-match speech is from Tom Humphries' *Irish Times* article 'Charlie's on and off day' (18/9/95). Charlie's post-match comments on his sending-off are from the same article. Other details on the match come from my interviews with Keith Barr, Charlie Redmond, Ciaran Walsh, Paddy Russell, Willie O'Mahony and Dessie Farrell.

Chapter Eight

Charlie's quote on the greatest of all Dublin teams comes from my interview with him. The account of the new management team's style comes from John O'Leary's and Dessie Farrell's autobiographies. The quote from Keith Barr on Meath is from Tom Humphries' *Irish Times* article 'Doctor lauds the benefits of new transfusion' (31/7/95), while other quotes are from my interview with him. Accounts of the aftermath of the final come from my interviews with Paddy Russell, Ciaran Walsh and Charlie Redmond.

Sources Used

Books, Articles and Extracts

Burke, R. *Press Delete: The Decline and Fall of the Irish Press* (Currach, Dublin, 2005)

Byrne, P. *Football Association of Ireland, 75 Years* (Sportsfile, Dublin, 1996)

Carey, T. *Croke Park: A History* (Collins Press, Cork, 2004)

Cronin, M. *Sport and Nationalism in Ireland: Gaelic Games, Soccer and Irish Identity since 1884* (Four Courts Press, Dublin, 1999)

de Búrca, M. *The GAA: A History*, 2nd edition (Gill and Macmillan, Dublin, 2000)

Doak, R. '(De)constructing Irishness in the 1990s – the Gaelic Athletic Association and Cultural Nationalist Discourse Reconsidered' in *Irish Journal of Sociology*, 8, pp. 35–6 (1998)

Doyle, R. 'Republic is a Beautiful Word – Republic of Ireland, 1990' in Hornby, N. (ed.) *My Favourite Year: A Collection of New Football Writing* (H.F. & G. Witherby, London, 1993)

Duggan, K. *The Lifelong Season* (Town House Press, Dublin, 2004)

Farrell, D. Dessie, *Tangled Up in Blue* (Town House Press, Dublin, 2005)

Hannigan, D. *The Garrison Game: The State of Irish Football* (Mainstream Publishing, Edinburgh, 1998)

Harnden, T. *'Bandit Country': The IRA and South Armagh* (Coronet/ Lir, London, 1999)

Healy, P. *The Search for Sam: The All-Ireland Football Championship '95* (Mercier Press, Dublin, 1995)

Holmes, M. 'Symbols of National Identity and Sport: The Case of the Irish Football Team' in *Irish Political Studies*, 9, pp. 81–98 (1993)

221

Houlihan, C. *More than a Game: Selected Sporting Essays* (Liberties Press, Dublin, 2003)

Humphries, T. *Green Fields: Gaelic Sport in Ireland* (Weidenfeld & Nicolson, London, 1996)

Keane, C. *Gaelic Football's Top 20* (Mainstream Publishing, Edinburgh, 2003)

Lanfranchi, P. 'Exporting Football: Notes on the Development of Football in Europe' in Giulianotti, R. and Williams, J. (eds) *Game Without Frontiers: Football, Identity and Modernity* (Ashgate Publishing Company, Aldershot, 1994)

Lee, J.J. *Ireland 1912–1985: Politics and Society* (Cambridge University Press, Cambridge, 1989)

Liddy, G.G. *Will* (Sphere Books, London, 1980)

Mahon, J. *A History of Gaelic Football* (Gill and Macmillan, Dublin, 2001)

McKay, S. *Northern Protestants: An Unsettled People* (Blackstaff Press, Belfast, 2000)

McKittrick, D., Kelters, S., Feeney, B. and Thornton, C. *Lost Lives* (Mainstream Publishing, Edinburgh, 1999)

O'Brien, M. *De Valera, Fianna Fáil and the Irish Press* (Irish Academic Press, Dublin, 2001)

Ó Hehir, M. *Micheal Ó Hehir: My Life and Times* (Blackwater Press, Dublin, 1996)

O'Leary, J. with Breheny, M. *Back to the Hill* (Blackwater Press, Dublin, 1997)

O'Rourke, C. *The Final Whistle* (Hero Books, Dublin, 1996)

Potts, S. *Páidí: The Life of Gaelic Football Legend Páidí Ó Sé* (Town House and Country House, Dublin, 2001)

Rafferty, E. *Talking Gaelic: Leading Personalities on the GAA* (Blackwater Press, Dublin, 1997)

Sugden, J. and Bairner, A. 'Ireland and the World Cup, "Two teams in Ireland, there's only two teams in Ireland . . ."' in Sugden, J. and Tomlinson, A. (eds) *Hosts and Champions: Soccer Cultures, National Identities and the USA World Cup* (Ashgate Publishing Company, Aldershot, 1994)

Sweeney, E. *The Road to Croker: A GAA Fanatic on the Championship Trail* (Hodder Headline Ireland, Dublin, 2004)

Tomlinson, A. 'North and South: The Football League and the Football Association' in Williams, J. and Wagg, S. (eds) *British Football and Social Change: Getting into Europe* (Leicester University Press, London, 1991)

Tomlinson, A. 'FIFA and the World Cup: The Expanding Football Family' in Sugden, J. and Tomlinson, A. (eds) *Hosts and Champions: Soccer Cultures, National Identities and the USA World Cup* (Ashgate Publishing Company, Aldershot, 1994)

Van Esbeck, E. *Irish Rugby 1874–1999: A History* (Gill and Macmillan, Dublin, 1999)

Newspapers
Evening Press (1974–9, 1983, 1991, 1995)
Irish Independent (1974–9, 1983, 1995)
Irish Times (1955, 1974–9, 1983, 1995)
XPress (1995)

Videos
The Dubs in the Rare Ould Times (produced by Brian O'Flaherty, RMG Entertainment Ltd, 2004)
Sam Returns to the Hill: The Gaelic Football Year 1995 (Stirling Films, Cumann Lúthchleas Gael and Sony Music, 1995)

Interviews
Keith Barr
Dessie Farrell
Willie O'Mahony
Charlie Redmond
Paddy Russell
Ciaran Walsh